BIRDWATCHING
for All Ages

—

Activities for Children and Adults

by Jorie Hunken

The
Globe
Pequot
press

Chester, Connecticut

About the Author

Jorie Hunken has been watching and listening to birds since her childhood in Georgia. The charm and beauty of birds were always a source of pleasure for her. Then as a teenager she saw birds die after eating caterpillars sprayed to protect the neighborhood trees. The next year her foundling baby robin died after eating earthworms from a mulch pile made of the sprayed leaves. Around that time Rachel Carson's *Silent Spring* was published. It explained how, in ways like these, human action poses a widespread threat to our birds and to ourselves. Finding effective ways to involve others in caring for what happens to the environment has since been Jorie's interest and career. *Birdwatching for All Ages* is a companion to her first book, *Botany for All Ages.*

Art credits: Pp. 38, 53, 152: John A. Lynch; pp. 18, 21 top: Heather Brack; p. 5: Evan Brack. All others by the author.

Library of Congress Cataloging-in-Publication Data

Hunken, Jorie.
    Birdwatching for all ages: Activities for children and adults / by Jorie Hunken.
— 1st ed.
        p. cm.
    Includes index.
    Summary: A birdwatching guide that explains how to find and observe birds in their natural habitats. Includes line drawings, photographs, and suggested activities.
    ISBN 0-87106-234-8
    1. Bird watching. 2. Birds. 3. Birds, Attracting of. [1. Bird watching. 2. Birds.]
I. Title.
QL677.5.H86 1992
598'.07'234—dc20
                           91-31566
                            CIP
                            AC

Book design by Nancy Freeborn
Manufactured in the United States of America
First Edition/Second Printing

Contents

Foreword

Birds—the image is of both beauty and freedom.

The behavior of birds and their natural history have fascinated men and women for centuries. Because of their worldwide distribution, birds have also become an important indicator species in the monitoring of the health of our environment.

Jorie Hunken has taken a subject with which she has intimate knowledge and shared that information, with all its wonder, in a comprehensive resource book on learning about birds. She has successfully combined the art and the science of birds and birding, uniting a sensitivity toward birds with the scientific information on their biology and behavior.

This is the perfect book for the layman who is looking for information on the natural history and behavior of birds but who is also interested in sharing that excitement and knowledge with children and others. I highly recommend this book as a way to get outside and experience nature and study nature firsthand. And who knows, by learning a little more about the natural world, we may learn a little more about ourselves.

Cleti Cervoni
Director of Education
Massachusetts Audubon Society

Thanks

This book comes out of a lifetime of watching birds. Along the way, special people have appeared and given direction to my journey. Without them the book would never have happened. All these people were teachers in some way, and since this book is about teaching, perhaps you will identify people like yourself in my list of acknowledgments.

Parents and siblings are role models. If they spend time outdoors, wonder over discoveries, and let children find their own ways, they influence children accordingly. I am very grateful to my parents for their support and to my sister for clearing the path before me.

Neighbors may have time or resources to support a child's growing interest. Walks with bird-loving neighbors and access to neighboring property provided me with important early learning experiences.

Most of my knowledge has come from books. I learned the call number for birds, 598.2, when I was eight and have since mined it like a vein of gold. Thank you, lending libraries everywhere.

A camp counselor at a summer camp may provide a child's first experience with someone who can interpret the natural environment. The model of teacher as learner can trigger a lifelong passion to learn. My thanks to the Nature Camp of Virginia and to my friend Henry Hespenheide.

Although it is the job of those who work at a nature center to educate the public, as models of caring, their effect can be enormous. I was deeply affected by Duryea Morton of the National Audubon Society when he was director of the Greenwich sanctuary. He taught me both birds and teaching.

The times when teachers acknowledged (and used) my love of nature to teach me to write or study biology or art were fabulous learning experiences. (For once they had my full attention, anyway.) My thanks to those teachers who believed in me as a learner. They are the reason I teach. You may already be using one of these modes as a means for expressing your interest in birds. Please keep on—teaching and learning and giving.

My thanks to the people who gave energy to the creation of this book. The editorial staff at Globe Pequot Press, specifically Laura Strom, made sure it all fit together. Cleti Cervoni and Widge Arms contributed ideas, as did, unknowingly, a number of curriculum writers whose material I found at The Hathaway Library at the Massachusetts Audubon Society. Dick Walton checked the natural history against his considerable store of information. Bernie McHugh and Carol Bershad lent me their computers and patiently taught me to use them. My family did a wonderful job of finding something else to do when I had to write or draw. My children, as with all children, always showed me what was important.

PART ONE

GETTING STARTED

Come as you are; look anywhere out-of-doors. Birds are everywhere. If there seem to be no birds, the bird you finally see must be very special. If birds are common, watch them long enough to learn something new. Seeing the new bird or the new behavior is what gets people hooked on birdwatching. You never know what will happen when you start out, but you will see something new every time.

Some people love to count all the species they have seen; the birds are a kind of wealth. Others hunt for the rarest find. Learning about bird behaviors gives us parallels to human behaviors. A knowledge of birds tells us about the health of our surroundings. The absence of a bird where a species should be is an indication that the environment is changing. These days, an endangered bird species probably means that people are endangering its habitat. The present decline in bird species means a loss of environmental diversity.

Knowing and watching birds is a joy. They are always more than pretty little things. They are more than environmental indicators or versions of our behavioral heritage. There is something about knowing birds that connects us to the deepest and loveliest patterns in nature. We are affected by their colors, their ways of flying, their songs, and the mysterious but steadfast rhythms of their migrations.

This book is a series of activities to help you expand upon your experiences with birds, either by yourself or with others. Concepts about the natural history of birds are explained in the context of projects to do, examples of behavior to watch for, and questions to think about and discuss. It is hoped that you will soon find your own way of enjoying birds and sharing your awareness with others.

For Teachers and Parents

Your Approach to Birdwatching

Birdwatching can be no more complicated than finding a bird and watching it for a while. Even common birds are interesting. If house sparrows and pigeons are all you have to work with, your interest might be stimulated if you were to learn their histories and interpretations of their behaviors. Whether teaching yourself or teaching others, begin with wild birds. Birds seen in zoos or books are not nearly as exciting as even a glimpse of a bird in its natural habitat. The outdoor sighting becomes a memory complete with spatial proportions, odors, and weather conditions. Set in so rich a matrix, information about the bird will be more accessible to recall, more valuable, and more a part of the viewer's life.

As you begin to find out about how individual birds look and act, seek some theme or goal to connect your experiences. You might begin with a diary of birds you've seen or drawings of your favorite species. Let you interests lead you on tangents. Do some habitats interest you more than others? Do certain behaviors catch your attention? As your study of birds continues, your ideas will change, and a record of those changes can be very satisfying. Some of the following activities might start out as minor disciplines, but they may lead to major involvements as birdwatching becomes a lifelong pleasure.

- Keep a journal of all the birds you see through the seasons, or record the seasonal activities of a favorite bird.

- Plan to write a book or magazine article. Researching and writing specific information, and being responsible for its accuracy, is a fine way to hone your knowledge.

- Draw birds until you can do it well. Make sketches of live birds or stuffed birds, or trace birds in photographs. Try to copy the work of other bird artists. Your efforts will result in keener observations.

- Keep checklists. State and national birdwatching organizations print lists of all birds native to particular areas. You might want to keep a life list, which includes all the birds you've seen in your life, or you might list all the birds you see on a vacation to a new area. You can also keep short lists for each year or season. Include the date and place that you saw each bird. The lists can be very interesting when compared in later years, both in showing changes in your birding abilities and changes in the habitats you once visited.

■ Make changes around your home to attract more species of birds. Many good books are available to guide you. Attracting birds with feeding stations, nest boxes, or just scattered bread crumbs will help you develop a personal relationship with local birds.

■ Let an interest in a particular bird draw you into learning about the environment in which it lives. Which plants are important to the bird's life? Which animals in the habitat affect the bird? Is the habitat likely to change, either because of natural succession or human development?

Just looking at pictures of birds is a kind of birdwatching. The amazing variety of birds' colors and shapes captivates even the smallest child.

Learning Modes

This book is about learning about birds. Because the goal of the book is to bring the most enjoyment and information to greatest number of new enthusiasts, it also explores the different processes people use to learn more about their environment. The activities in the book are designed to be useful and interesting to groups of children who may learn in different ways.

    If you find you are drawn to certain kinds of activities, it may be because the activities incorporate learning modes that are comfortable for you. Which of the following activities have the greatest appeal to you?

■ Keeping lists of all the species of birds you see over a year.

■ Going on vacation just to see some rare birds to add to your list.

■ Spending time in the outdoors to find out what birds are there and what they are doing.

- Picking a bird with characteristics that appeal to you and thinking of it as your personal symbol.

- Using bird features in graphics, music, drama, or writing to convey feelings and ideas.

The activities you chose may be similar to other kinds of activities you do; most likely they reflect the way you usually operate. You can probably pick out the activities certain friends would prefer, relative to their usual habits or activities. For hobbies especially, people tend to enjoy certain kinds of procedures or modes more than others.

Scientists have discovered that these modes can be characterized and sorted into two categories analogous to the functions of the left and right brain lobes. The left brain is primarily responsible for logical and linear thought processes. The right brain seeks out patterns, especially spatial relationships, and the processes seem more random and radiating in function. The initial research that led scientists to these distinctions involved people whose connecting tissue between the lobes had been damaged. In these individuals, the two modes functioned separately, sometimes defensively, in relation to each other. For most people, the functions are integrated, and we can be logical and goal-oriented or pattern-finding and feeling-oriented as we need. If a person could be only one mode or the other, he or she could be described as follows:

Logical/Linear

When operating in left-brain mode, individuals are characterized by a verbal, logical, goal-oriented style. They enjoy detail and like to be correct; they follow directions and rules and are math-oriented; they appreciate the organization of music and other controlled art forms. The skills they contribute to an activity enable them to organize a complicated problem so that it can be processed, solved, or communicated.

Typical L/L-enhancing activities are:

- Listing and sorting attributes and learning terms for describing details

- Participating in competitive games, such as scavenger hunts, that lead to a goal

- Detecting clues and solving mysteries

- Creating art for the sake of reproducing an image accurately

- Stencilling shapes and coloring within the lines

- Completing other activities that demand skills in counting, describing, comparing, predicting, or critiquing.

Copying birds from pictures can teach the artist a great deal about the shapes and postures of birds. The resulting picture can be very lovely, too.

Random/Radiating

When operating in a right-brain mode, individuals are characterized by a sensitivity to sensate information and to the patterns created by movement, sound, and colors. They have an awareness of the interrelationships between dissimilar objects or events. They project subjective characteristics onto objects and can tolerate disorder (new relationships, for example, are usually discovered through random action). They enjoy outrageous connections and outcomes and are more satisfied by a new perception than an external goal. The skills they contribute enable them to intuit possible directions for investigation, discern overall patterns, and solve problems by comparing analogous processes.

Typical R/R-enhancing activities are:

- Creating art for the sake of illustrating a new concept

- Putting together words in new ways for a fresh perspective

- Playing games that make associations between items

- Participating in group activities such as creating a poem, play, or mural

- Bringing in and describing discoveries

- Completing activities that require skills in imagining, projecting possibilities, finding analogies, and making metaphors.

Parents and teachers influence the modes we use. An environment that relies on books for information and written tests for evaluation develops only the left side of the brain. People who are more comfortable with right-side modes may find themselves steered toward an education in manual arts or other undervalued "artsy-craftsy" pursuits. Parents, teachers, and others who care for very young children know that most individuals have a natural tendency to use one mode more readily than the other. The ideal learning situation incorporates both modes of operating so that each child has a chance to shine and a chance to learn.

As you learn and as you share your knowledge, make a conscious effort to use both learning modes, even if a particular activity is not appealing to you. Consider it an exercise in flexing unused brain modes. A sample activity based on chicken eggs follows. It includes suggestions for integrating the two learning modes. Try to use this "two-handed," double-brained approach as you do the other activities in the book. By approaching a topic with logic as well as the senses, using both critical as well as imaginative skills, both teacher and students will learn more and express more.

Chicken Eggs

- Investigate the attributes of the parts, then name and describe their relationships.

   1) Crack an egg into a shallow bowl and examine each part. Describe the qualities of each.

   2) Take apart a hard-boiled (10-minute) egg for a better idea of the positions and relative amounts of the parts. (See section on eggs, beginning on page 44.)

- Experiment with the parts, investigating the qualities and uses of each. Ask questions and brainstorm various possible functions. Create tests, discuss results, and consider further testing.

   1) Spin both fresh and hard-boiled eggs and describe differences in responses. What factors might be influencing the raw egg's shorter spinning time? (Helpful analogy: spinning ice skaters extend their arms to slow their spin. The dense, off-center yolk is pulled out to one end by the spinning motion, and the egg slows.)

   2) Try to break a fresh egg by squeezing it in one hand. (It's especially difficult when squeezed end to end.) Compare by squeezing a hard-boiled egg and discuss possible reasons for the different response.

   3) The calcium of the shell is affected by acids, such as vinegar. Soak an egg overnight in vinegar and compare it with an unsoaked egg. Try soaking in vinegar for longer periods. Does vinegar make the shell softer or thinner? What other experiments can you do with shells and acid?

■ Use the experiences as the basis of more investigations and to make new creations.

1) Find out how eggs are cooked and used, especially in other cultures. China's "Thousand Year Old Eggs," for instance, are among the interesting recipes for eggs.

2) Teach someone else what you know about eggs. Write a book of experiments for others to try. Make drawings showing egg parts.

3) Read books on Eastern European egg art traditions and try to create some similar egg art projects of your own.

4) Other art techniques use eggs as materials. A long-lasting paint is made by mixing colors with fresh yolk. In another process, pieces of shells are pasted inside-up on wood to create a gleaming, crackly "canvas."

5) Make up new kinds of animals, plants, cars, machines, or buildings using only egg shapes (drawn or made from clay, papier mâché, egg cartons, or stocking containers).

6) Read creation myths of various cultures; many use eggs as symbols of the "Beginning." Create your own myth using a magical egg. Imagine the characters in rich detail and create puppets to act out the story.

7) See the sections on camouflage and the effect of habitat for other ideas pertaining to eggs.

Hints for Teaching the Activities in This Book

■ All the activities in this book should begin with a discussion or a listing game (see Basic Strategy for Careful Observation, page 10) to find out what each child or student already knows about birds. This sharing process is essential for learning. The learner starts out with some sense of authority, of knowing something, and the teacher learns where to start offering new experiences. Interaction is better in small groups in which the learners can experience from the outset the positive feeling of contributing and learning on a peer level. Most birdwatchers would agree that their pleasures come from the special interplay of personal experience (the sighting) given value by group appreciation.

■ Do not begin to study birds with a study of parts or concepts. Begin by discussing the attributes of birds the group knows. Exercises or activities on subjects such as camouflage or bird bills will mean more if the children use birds they already know.

Discovering birds with a friend or sharing the experiences of solitary discoveries is one of the pleasures of being a birdwatcher.

- Make connections between birds and the established interests of the group. Kids are already proficient students of such details as trivia relating to current sport, cartoon, and movie characters. Relate bird details to similar characteristics the children will recognize (which birds are jet planes; which are fashionable dressers?).

- Many teachers concur that a predetermined goal, a clipboard, and a pencil are very helpful for settling and focusing children on an outdoor excursion. The birds can be counted, described, or sorted under behavioral headings. One bird can be followed for five minutes, or a single area can be monitored for a set time. If the children are not used to being outdoors, it is especially important to establish set limits on what is to be observed and for how long.

- Focus on birds that are residents in familiar places. Be on the lookout for birds along your daily routes. You will discover that once you become aware of birds, they seem to be everywhere. Where you thought there was only noise, there is song; where you thought the landscape was empty, birds are busy.

- Your delight and interest in birds will be the best encouragement for beginning birdwatchers, especially children. You don't have to try to sound like a bird authority. Let the children know that you are learning about birds too and that you are excited by your knowledge. Invite them to learn along with you. Make sure that children understand that you learned from other people and that you are simply passing on the ideas. Give the children the notion that they are teachers also; whatever they learn they can teach to others.

Children learn best through pleasant shared experiences: Even a brief tickle with a beautiful feather can start a string of happy memories of enjoying birds.

- Talk about the children's feelings about birds. Find out if there are birds that the children already know or love or dislike. Talk about why people might have different feelings about different birds. Ask for stories (real or imagined) about people feeling strongly about a kind of bird. Look at illustrations or paintings of birds. (Look for a variety of bird and wildlife artists. Illustrations by Audubon, Bates, Fuertes, or Peterson are probably in your library.) Using pictures that seem to tell a story, ask for ideas about what is happening in a painting. Talk about the choices the artist made to express his or her feelings about the birds. Encourage the children to make drawings that show their feelings about birds.

- Use art whenever possible as a means of enhancing observation skills and to encourage self-expression relative to the new experiences and ideas. Make drawings; paintings; computer printouts; cut-outs or stencils; models from clay, papier-mâché, or balsa wood; designs in beads and mosaics, for quilts, or in collages made with recycled materials. The simple shape of a flying bird is attainable for the youngest artist. Older children may want to recreate the intricacy of detail in a single bird.

- Puppets can be used to animate the illustration. The combination of created form and personal animation increases personal involvement exponentially. Cut-outs can be taped to sticks to make lively movements. (For younger participants, attach the bird to the stick with a length of string or thread. Movements must be slower to be birdlike, and this inhibition may reduce some of the tendency to whip the stick around.) Animation leads to storytelling. Let the stories emerge from the children's movements or start the story with a simple event. What might happen during one day in a bird's life? How would the bird move when searching for food, when courting, or when fleeing? What is happening in the nearby environment that could be used in your story? Remember that a bird puppet has a special magic feature: a voice. What would the bird like to tell us now that it can speak?

■ As you work with children, make sure they feel that they can identify a bird incorrectly without any embarrassment or loss of self-esteem. What they claim to see or what they think will happen should only open up non-authoritative debate. ("You think you saw a flock of California condors along the New Jersey Turnpike? Could they have been any other kind of vulture?") The children's thoughts and feelings must be allowed to develop on their own, as long as their ideas do not lead to injury to self or others.

The activities in the chapters that follow are meant to expand children's awareness of the natural world and strengthen their relationship to it. By knowing birds, by knowing *about* birds, we learn to understand the interconnectedness of people and birds and of all the lives around us.

Basic Strategy for Careful Observation

Mythical Argus was known as a sharp-eyed and thorough observer. Having a thousand eyes was his main asset, each eye giving him a slightly different perspective on the scene. This Argus Effect can be duplicated by several people sharing their observations. Whether the "thing observed" is a feather or a view of a habitat, as each person in turn describes one aspect, all observers collect a new sight. The effect is self-enhancing. Having to pick a new attribute to describe makes the observer look more carefully and at the same time increases the number of things seen and described. The group's vocabulary is also expanded. (Although it is tempting to introduce new words during the description process, the effect of "correcting" with the "proper" word may smother the group's creativity and willingness to perceive new aspects. Appreciate and use the children's original wording and save unfamiliar terminology for later discussions.)

If the object to be observed can be safely handled, structure the process by forming a circle so that the object can be passed around the circle. Give each person time to find a new aspect to describe and, as the leader, try to give each response an equal value. You may find that a low-key response works best. Show your enthusiasm for the group as a whole at the end. If observations slacken, change the point of view. The object might be turned around and magnifying glasses or reversed binoculars used to give close-up views. Or look closely at the object through a small opening made by the thumb and index finger. To bring out new attributes, ask what the object resembles or what it might be used for.

If the descriptions are written down as they are said, the observations

A simple feather seems full of interesting attributes when people take turns describing their observations. After every feature has been noted, try thinking of how a feather might be useful, based on the features mentioned.

are given a greater value. Each contributor feels his or her offering is worthwhile and is more likely to want to say more. The words and phrases might also be used to create descriptive writing, poems, and so on. The group process models an important discipline for individuals as well. Some of the same effects work for a solitary observer: noting an aspect, writing it down, and sharing it with others.

Playing with Ideas about Birds

The following activities can be used to enhance observation and communication skills and as strategies for integrating art, language, and science. If you are involved in working with children as a teacher, parent, or camp counselor, you might find them adaptable to work you are already doing. They assume an ability to read and write in the participants, but they can easily be adapted to preliterate children by using spoken responses. They are also appropriate for faster-moving camp or party games. Several would be good to use as games while waiting or traveling.

■ **Guess What Bird I Am:** The name of a known bird is selected for or by a player, and others must guess its identity. The guessers will be more challenged if questions may only be answered yes or no. A variation: The names are taped on the backs of the players and they must ask questions to find out their identity. A group can play all at once if questions are asked by taking turns so that everyone finishes at about the same time.

■ **Habitat Hob-Nob:** List by turns a sequence of bird behaviors that would be typical of a particular habitat. Begin with a brief phrase that includes the habitat ("I was standing in a meadow, and what did I see..."), and then add names of birds and describe their possible (or observed) activities ("a field sparrow building its nest in the grass," "a kestrel hovering high in the air"). This activity works nicely as a summary for a visit to a variety of habitats. Groups might work independently, then combine their efforts. Illustrations could be added.

■ **Bird News:** Write up descriptions of bird sightings as though they were newspaper articles. Include distinctive markings on the birds, what they were doing, and any other significant aspects. Include illustrations with captions.

■ **Cinquains:** This highly stylized form of poetry lends itself very well to short descriptions of bird behavior. It can also be done in groups. Each person contributes several descriptive words or phrases and the group fits the results into the cinquain format. The format is as follows:

- A single word (the species name) as a title
- Two-word description (how the bird looks)
- Three words describing the action (what the bird is doing)
- Four words interpreting the feeling or meaning, perhaps an analogy
- Back to one word to sum up the impression

> An example is :
>
> Chickadee
> Brave thumbkin
> Wins over winter
> Singing in the sunshine
> Solo

■ **Bird Myths:** Read myths of various cultures to find those that involve birds. Do any stories use behaviors that you know to be authentic, or are the birds behaving as though they were people? Make up some myths of your own using bird behavior you know to be true. Create illustrations that show your bird transformed into a mythical creature.

■ **Charades:** Pantomime known birds with distinctive behaviors. The traditional set-up of a charade game is for one group to tell a member of another group which item is to be acted out. The member must then go back to his or her group and communicate the word or phrase using only gestures. The charade tactic of suggesting the bird by a rhyme of its name might be used. (The gesture for "sounds like" is a pull on the ear. Make up your own signals to show the number of words in the name, or syllables in a word.)

■ **Bird Riddles:** Make up riddles using the names of birds . . . the sillier the better. "What bird danced with the fiddle while another bird jumped over

Emma draws a princess bird.

the moon?" (Catbird, Cowbird.) "What's a bird to describe a madly shouting crow?" (A Raven.) "What would a rhymer call a woodpecker's raincoat?" (A Flicker's Slicker.)

- **Bird Poll:** Interview a series of people (even ones that don't know many birds) to find out what they do know or feel about birds. Examples might be: Which bird would you like to be? What's the silliest bird? What's the rarest bird? What could be done to save it? Where do most birds live?

- **Alien Birdlife:** Find out about the climates of other planets and design space birds that could live there. Use real birds that live in extreme climates on earth as models for your alien creations.

- **Birds and People:** Birds have been used by people as food, clothing, decoration, pets, and as symbols of power, mystery, or humor. Look through anthropology texts, *National Geographic* and *Smithsonian* magazines, art books, encyclopedias, and so on for illustrations and descriptions of bird uses in various cultures. Which birds have special meaning for you? How

It feels special to wear bird feathers. Even ones off a feather duster have some of the magic of winged creatures of flight.

would you express your attitudes? Are there characteristics that you would claim or emulate? (Note: Federal law prohibits individuals from collecting wild bird feathers and having them in their possession.)

- **Grocery Store Bird Watching:** Make a list of any birds or products using bird parts to be found in a market. Eggs as ingredients will be the most numerous, perhaps limit the listing to food names instead of ingredient lists.

- **Flights of Fancy:** A bird's ability to fly provides it with experiences we can only imagine. Do just that; imagine episodes of flight for different species of birds. The best creations will be based on observations of real birds. Make notes in the field, follow birds around if possible, then write up the notes into stories.

- **State Birds:** The study of the list of state birds can give some idea of ranges of various birds, because favorite birds common to some states may not be found in other states. The listing, however, is more likely to represent regional tastes in birdlife than ranges. It might be interesting to discuss possibilities as to why particular birds were selected as state birds. To get an idea of the process involved, members of a family or class might nominate favorite birds as the class or family bird. Reasons could then be put forward justifying the selection. (Posters, news profiles, advertisements?) Decide as a class how the final decision will be made.

PART TWO

FIRST EXPERIENCES

I don't know any child who doesn't collect things, stuff, and memories. It seems to be a human response to the world: to pick out a theme and collect facts and items that relate to it. There is often a curious sense of connectedness as one event leads to a greater awareness of possibilities.

The activities in this chapter are meant to increase those possibilities for the beginning collector of bird experiences. They've been chosen to appeal to diverse backgrounds and learning styles. (Some people have to have pictures, some people have to have words.) You will find that some children don't see the birds at first because they aren't used to being outdoors. The effects of the wind, sun, and trees are too distracting; the feeling of open space too unfamiliar or too stimulating.

Always start with the children's own experiences and build from that point. Find out what they already know and take them outside as often as possible. Don't expect children to take the lead or explore in ways you think they should. Demonstrate your interest, initiate the activities yourself, and invite the kids to play with you. Soon the children will be enticed to learn on their own.

Activities Using General Concepts about Birds

Using a Bird Book

It's possible to learn to identify species of birds both by observing live ones and by looking at illustrations. A picture page of warblers, sparrows, ducks, or thrushes can show the range of variations and the distinctions between each variety. The field guide pictures alone can impart some information that may prove helpful in the field. The following activities are useful to help familiarize children with books on birds and with the birds themselves.

A single feather can often be identified by scanning the pictures in a bird book. In this case, the yellow of the feather shaft identifies the feather as belonging to the northern flicker.

■ Start a life list. Write down which birds you have seen so far. Look through the illustrations to find any others you know you have seen before. Write down where you saw the bird for the first time and, if possible, the date on which you saw it. (Some bird books have a list in the front just for checking off life birds.) Seasonal lists can be of interest. Early or late arrivals of migrating flocks might relate to weather conditions; or a single straggler at the "wrong" season might be of more interest than a flock when expected.

■ Some of the terms used to describe body areas on a bird may be new to beginning birders. All the field guides have illustrations with labeled parts in their introductory pages. Make a game of learning the terms by having one person point to an area on his or her body while others try to name the comparable area on a bird.

■ Even if you can't yet identify any birds, lists of species with distinctive characteristics can be compiled by thumbing through a guide (a good group activity). Here are a few suggestions:

- List birds with bills longer than their heads.

- List birds with white patches on wing or tail feathers. (By fanning the feathers, the white patches might be used as signals. See page 73)

- What families of birds are mostly camouflaged? List examples.

- What species show similarities in coloration? List examples.

- Find all the birds starting with a particular first initial.

- Which bird has the largest eyes? The longest tail?

- Find the smallest bird; find the largest.

- List birds that are named for their call or song.

- If the bird book shows range maps, which birds can be found on both the East and West coasts?

- Which species have different plumages for male and female birds?

■ Make up a new kind of bird, using parts of at least three different birds. Give it a name and describe how it gets its food.

■ Use a design of your own to create plumage patterns. (Warblers, sparrows, thrushes, and orioles are good models.) Check out designs on butterflies, tropical fish, or flowers and apply them to birds.

■ Make a list of birds everyone knows, then look carefully at their illustrations for some visible but inconspicuous characteristic. Challenge another person to identify a bird by its more obscure markings. (For example, robins have black and white stripes on their throats.)

■ Look through the bird book for bird names with interesting descriptive adjectives, such as pied-billed grebe, scissor-tailed flycatcher, and three-toed woodpecker. Apply the terms to other birds. (What would a scissor-tailed cardinal look like?) Draw the new bird.

■ Choose a favorite bird and write up an interview with it. Ask questions about the bird's life and use the book to look up its "answers." Whenever possible, include information or behaviors you have actually observed.

**A cartoon creation of a "dis-
posable razor-bill auk."**

- If you have access to a book with pictures of birds interacting in some way, write a story describing the event. Audubon's *Birds of America* is especially good. Even in those illustrations that show no story, use the setting for an event of your own invention. Write the story from the observer's or the bird's point of view.

- In the old word game, "In My Grandmother's Trunk," a list of items is created by starting with a noun beginning with an *A*, and adding a second item beginning with a *B*, and so on, through the alphabet. The entire list has to be repeated correctly by each player before he or she can add a new item. Birdwatchers can play "In My Grandmother's Mistnet," using bird names for the alphabetized items. You may want to include non-native birds for the harder letters. If the players are beginners, allow them to make a written list and refer to bird books for possibile answers.

- In a slightly more advanced game than the preceding version, a bird is chosen at random, and the last letter of its name must be the first for the next bird and so on. It's interesting to have two groups work separately and compare results.

- Draw a set of bird pictures on index cards for simple games. The easiest method is to create a set of duplicate pictures for games such as "Go Fish," "Concentration," or "Slap Jack." Make up appropriate names for your new bird games.

Becoming a Bird

What might it be like to be a bird? By asking the children to choose the kinds of birds they want to be, the characteristics of birds become personal knowledge, and the lives of birds become more concrete. Choose a number of familiar birds of different shapes, sizes, and ways of moving. It isn't necessary to pretend to be a particular species. The children can choose general categories, combining the shared characteristics of several species. Look through a bird identification book for your geographical area for examples of species with like features. The following ideas will get you started:

- *Daytime hunter:* Soaring wings; flesh-tearing beak; strong talons for grasping and tearing; keen eyesight. (Hawks, eagles, falcons)

- *Nighttime hunter:* Soft wing feathers for hushed flight; tearing beak; strong, grasping talons; large eyes for night vision; keen hearing. (Owls)

- *Ground-dwelling seed and insect eater:* Short, curved wings for rapid get away; pecking bill; strong feet for scratching the ground for food. (Turkeys, grouse, pheasants, quail)

- *Water wader:* Long legs with wide-spread toes for balance; long bill for catching water creatures; stealthy movements; sharp eyes. (Herons, storks, cranes)

- *Seed eater:* Small size for perching on plants; thick bill for cracking seeds; bright colors for attracting birds of its own kind; feeds in flocks for safety. (Sparrows, finches, juncos)

- *Sipper of flower nectar:* Long bill and tongue for collecting nectar from flowers; small, slender wings; zippy movements; brilliant, reflective color patches for startling enemies. (Hummingbirds)

- *Insect catcher:* Strong, long wings for tight maneuvers; keen eyesight; long tail feathers for steering and balance; wide mouth with slightly hooked bill. (Flycatchers, swallows)

You can best judge the method of offering the choices. If sketches accompany the general descriptions, visually oriented and younger children will feel more comfortable. More experienced children might be able to get started right from the descriptions, creating their own versions. You might refer to actual birds in illustrations before starting to work, or you might wait to make the connections when the activity is over. Assess the children's readiness to work. If they hesitate for lack of images, refer to actual birds as examples. Encourage acting out the movements of the chosen bird types. How might the bird act? What noises would it make? (As this is an imaginary bird, whatever a child decides is right.)

The creations can take many forms. The birds can be sketched and colored, assembled from cut-out parts, mounted on sticks or strings for more dramatic movement, or made as puppets using fabric or papier-mâché. You might even try whole costumes, with bird masks on faces and bird wings on arms.

The greater the involvement, the greater the knowledge gained. Encourage other activities with the bird models, such as the creation of stories about the birds. You may have to make up your own story as a model. Take the children on an imaginary journey through the eyes of a bird. The children's stories might use the context of a typical day, a day of crisis (a

In the process of making bird masks or costumes, the maker must become a bird to some extent. If the maker and performer incorporate the forms and movements of real birds, a wonderful magic occurs.

storm or confronting a predator), a life history, or a mythical event (offer Native American or African folk tales as examples). Once the character and behavior of each bird has been established, older children might be able to work out a play including all the birds. Having the birds explain environmental problems such as habitat loss due to blundering humans works very well as a theme. Kids relish setting grown-ups straight.

The goal in these activities is to involve each child in the life of a bird, real or imaginary, as long as the pretend bird is based on a real bird. Children are full of strong feelings that puppet-play can sometimes accentuate. Our most powerful myths are combinations of natural history and human feelings.

Bird News

We're all familiar with the television jargon of a television news broadcast. It might sound like: "This morning, (someone) was seen (doing something) near (somewhere)." The significance of the event is then described, and the final comment is expressed as an opinion or a query. Encourage the children to listen to the way news is presented and challenge them to report on their bird observations using the same style. It's best to have the kids first analyze the structure of a broadcast. Discuss the most common elements with them and help them organize their information. Their observations should include the identity of the bird, its identifying characteristics, when and where it was seen, a clear description of what it was doing, and guesses as to how its behavior relates to its life events or the season.

Newspapers that cover the news of a large district often group events by their locale. After collecting a number of reports on bird events, sort them into habitat groupings. This sorting might help you find the birds again and calls attention to the important connection between the lives of birds and their particular habitats.

"The jousting club is proud to welcome Sir Pintail of the Marsh."

Bird Cartoons

Creating cartoons of talking birds is a great way to involve kids' imaginations. (Their caricatures should be based on real birds, but they don't have to look real.) The goal of the activity is for kids to figure out what the birds might say in response to some factor in their environment: changes in the weather, family events, growing up, or problems created by humans (pollution, development, etc.). This last category is invariably interesting. Putting words in the mouths of birds gives children a chance to express their own feelings.

If the children want to make their cartoon birds look like actual birds, use the shapes in the following illustrations as a basis for more realistic bodies.

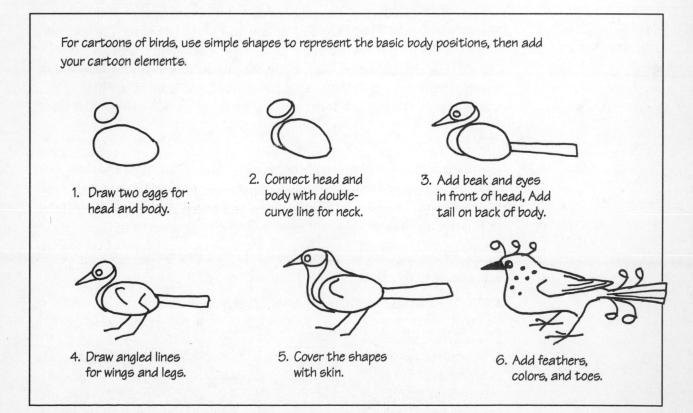

For cartoons of birds, use simple shapes to represent the basic body positions, then add your cartoon elements.

1. Draw two eggs for head and body.

2. Connect head and body with double-curve line for neck.

3. Add beak and eyes in front of head. Add tail on back of body.

4. Draw angled lines for wings and legs.

5. Cover the shapes with skin.

6. Add feathers, colors, and toes.

Sayings about Birds

As your study of birds proceeds, begin to collect sayings referring to birds. Introduce the idea with a discussion of some common sayings. Mention phrases such as "Don't count your chickens before they're hatched," "The early bird catches the worm," or "They're just feathering their own nest." Ask the children to name the human behaviors they think are being described. Do the sayings tell us anything about actual bird life? Accept the children's responses without criticism. This is a good way to find out what they know about birds (much of their "knowledge" may be based on the misinformation of common idioms). Note their general misconceptions as areas for further investigation. As new experiences and ideas are presented, refer to the sayings for an updated analysis. It might be fun to have each saying illustrated with a cartoon of a bird doing the action. Make a list of bird names used to describe human attributes, such as "happy as a lark" and "henpecked."

Memories of Birds

Birds so abound in the world that they can be seen every place that people live. We all have memories of birds, even if some of the images come from television. Spend some time discussing what birds the children have seen themselves and how they were acting. Don't try to edit the descriptions for accuracy; try to draw out a number of different bird behaviors and build a shared vocabulary describing bird actions and bird body parts. List each bird activity and group them according to stages of a general life history. Stages can include nests and eggs, baby birds, feeding behaviors, flying behaviors, survival behaviors, and death. After the group has a sense of the life experience of birds, add to their understanding by using the following activities.

 TO DO

Choose a bird species known to the children and discuss the behaviors they have seen. After collecting several anecdotes, try to relate them to a general life history of the bird. Use illustrations and books to add missing information. Try to collect memories or images of each of the following:

- Hatching from an egg and being cared for by a parent bird

- Learning to fly and to find food and shelter

- Keeping safe and getting away from dangerous situations

- Finding a mate and a place to build a nest and raise young

- Dying (it is likely that some children will have mentioned finding a dead bird).

After the special aspects of a bird's life are clear to the group, the information can be expressed in a number of ways. Each child can describe a specific life event, or each can illustrate or write a story of the bird's whole life. These histories can also be presented orally. The goal is to involve each child in ideas about birds. Encourage vivid descriptions of the scenes and actions. This activity can be repeated as the children gain more information and add it to their stories. Referring to this exercise at a later time is a good way for the children to compare what they knew at the beginning with all they have learned since.

■ Make a chart or worksheets with categories for listing bird events. Add to the list over a period of time. The most valuable categories will come from the children as they observe bird behaviors, but you can start the ball rolling with these ideas: birds seen from windows, birds up close, birds being noisy, birds getting food, birds singing. If particular habitats are noticed regularly, be sure to include them as categories. For example, kids might list birds on a ledge, birds in a tree, or birds under roof eaves. The concept of habitat is important in understanding any bird behavior.

■ To encourage descriptive imagery, create a bird poem. Begin the poem with the phrase "I've seen a bird . . ." and add the images of reported bird events. A group can contribute individual descriptions, a bird life history can be described, or a day of birding can be summarized. Repeat the opening phrase at the end with an appropriate closing image.

Activities Using Commonly Found Items

Dead Birds—What Can You See?

Observation of a dead bird can be a good introduction to the study of birds. Causes of bird death can be discussed, and interesting details of bird anatomy can be discovered. Examination of a dead bird also provides an opportunity to talk about the process of decay and natural recycling. (Adults should keep in mind that there are strict Federal laws regarding the possession of living or dead wild birds. Special licenses are required for people who keep such collections.)

It's not a good idea to let children handle a dead bird, especially if you are not sure how it died. There are very few diseases that people can contract from wild-living birds, but young children are likely to put their fingers in their mouths and noses, and even the remote possibility of disease must be avoided. You may wish to wear gloves as you handle the bird and make a point of thorough hand-washing when finished.

An adult group leader should handle the dead bird with gentleness and respect to help the children approach the activity with interest instead of fear. Make sure everyone is able to see the bird. The questions will come quickly from the children. They will be very interested to know how the bird died, so deal with that issue thoroughly before trying to talk about anatomy or other topics. With young children, direct their attention to differences between the bird's body and their own bodies ("Do birds have hair, toes, hands, mouths? Can they smile? How do they get around?"). Ask the children what they have seen of birds ("Where have you seen birds? What were they doing? Can birds talk? What have you seen them eat? How do birds move when they are on the ground?"). Encourage the children to show with their own gestures the actions they have seen birds do.

A good icebreaker and vocabulary-building activity is to ask each participant to name one detail about the bird. The physical presence of the bird might serve to inspire some imaginative storytelling or drawing. Ask for stories about some aspect of the life (or death) of this bird. Sketches can be made of the dead bird, or it can be drawn as it might have looked when alive. The process of drawing the bird is invaluable practice in looking carefully at all birds. Note that although all of these activities can be done without identifying the bird, this is an excellent opportunity to use a field guide and to try to find identifying characteristics.

Disposing of the body is certain to be an issue with the children. Ask them for suggestions and discuss the possibilities as a group. If possible, steer them toward a burial that allows for the natural process of decay, but respect the flourishes that help them express their feelings for the bird they have come to know.

Feathers

Before discussing a bird's use of its feathers, ask the children for examples of ways feathers are used by people. They may know about feather dusters, down stuffing in winter jackets, quilts, and pillows, or they may have seen feathers as fishing lures or decorations on hats. By searching through books on native peoples, you may find examples of feathers used as ceremonial or status objects. Try to find an illustration of a person writing with a quill ink pen; most elementary-school history books include an illustration of the signing of the Declaration of Independence, for instance. Talk about how it must have been to write with quill pens: Where would the ink be kept? How would the tip stay sharp? Where could a person find replacements?

Before you start looking for feathers, make a list of possible sources of feathers. A trip through a shopping mall, a hardware store, or a department store should turn up a number of feathers in various uses. Write down all the items that use feathers and list them according to uses—decoration, insulation, cleaning, and so on.

Federal law prohibits people from collecting feathers of wild birds. These laws are important because they protect our birds from people who would kill birds for their feathers. You and the children should talk about what might happen if there were no restrictions on collecting feathers. Mention the effect of turn-of-the-century hat fashions, when terns and egrets were slaughtered for their wings and plumes. What would happen as the birds became overhunted and rare? If people wanted to pay high prices for rare feathers, would the hunters stop hunting the rare birds?

Most of the feathers found in stores are from game birds that have been raised in captivity for their feathers, meat, or eggs. Pheasants, peacocks, ducks, geese, turkeys, and various types of chickens provide us with a useful and colorful array of feathers. The brightly colored feathers on toys, for instance, are usually dyed chicken feathers.

The longest and strongest bird feathers have traditionally been used for such items as pen quills and Native American decorations. A bird uses these feathers for flying and steering. You are most likely to notice these feathers on the ground outside, where they have fallen from the wings and tails of wild birds. Crow and jay feathers are commonly found.

"Feather duster" feathers are usually coverings for the body and upper legs of birds such as chickens and turkeys. They overlap like shingles on the roof of a house and shed water and dirt in a similar way. These feathers are softer than flight feathers and are more curved. Usually only the tip end is colorful, and it is the only part that shows. The fluffier parts are next to the bird's body and help provide insulation from cold or heat. Little muscles at the base of each feather allow the stalk of the feather to be raised slightly for display or to fluff up the covering for extra warmth.

The softest and fluffiest feathers, the down used for winter coats and vests, grow most thickly on birds that live in cold climates, especially water birds such as geese, ducks, and penguins. All baby birds have down feathers as their first outfits. The furry-looking baby down is thickest on chicks and ducklings—babies that care for themselves soon after hatching.

 TO DO

- Pass around a feather or a variety of feathers. Spend some time playing with them: Tickle with them, ruffle and smooth them, and use them for fans. Then take turns describing the attributes of each feather. You might want to keep a list of features. What colors are on the feather? Are the colors on both sides? Are the colors still visible when held up against the light? What adjectives describe the different parts? Where is the feather stiff, flexible, soft, round, or flat? What other object is like a feather?

- Have the children record their feather observations in a poem form. Start with "Like a ( ), a feather is (list descriptive adjectives . . .)" and end with "a feather is like a (same as above)." Each participant can write his or her own poem, or the group can write one poem together.

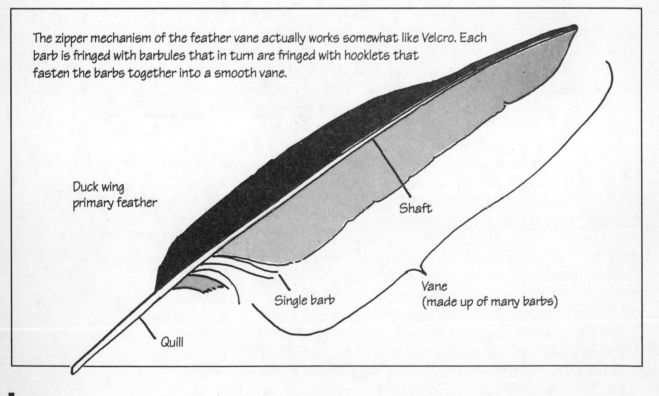

The zipper mechanism of the feather vane actually works somewhat like Velcro. Each barb is fringed with barbules that in turn are fringed with hooklets that fasten the barbs together into a smooth vane.

Duck wing
primary feather

Shaft

Single barb

Vane
(made up of many barbs)

Quill

■ Have the group continue to examine feathers while you introduce information on the colors of feathers. Bird feathers are usually differently colored on their upper and lower sides. Some of the colors are the result of pigments, which are particles of color embedded in the surface of the feather in much the same way our skin is pigmented. Other colors, the gleaming blues and greens especially, can be seen when sunlight flashes off rows of prismlike structures on the feather. Like the bright tints on the edges of crystals and the surface of soap bubbles, the colors are the products of bent light rays. The light is said to be refracted. Have the children hold the feathers up so that the light passes through them. If the effect is different from when they looked down on the feather, if the bright colors seem to disappear, then the bright colors are the result of refraction, not reflection. This capacity for "color at will" allows a bird to hide from danger by moving away from the light into the shadows or to impress a mate or startle a rival by facing the light for a brightly gleaming display.

The feathers of wing tips or tail are often dark colors. The dark pigment, melanin, gives strength to the important feathers of flight.

■ Try some other ways to test for pigments versus refracted colors. Dip a feather in salad oil; refracted colors will be masked by the oil. You can also break the prism structures by hammering the feather with a stone or a spoon to erase the effect of the refracted light.

■ Discuss the bird behavior of preening and feather straightening. A bird spends much of its waking day preening, or smoothing and arranging its feathers. One feather after another is drawn through its tightly clamped bill. Give each child a chance to "preen a feather." Using their fingernails as bills, they should draw the blade of a disrupted feather (flight feathers work the best) through their thumb and index fingers. The rough, zipperlike edges that hold a feather to its shape will adhere when tightly pressed. Ask the children if they know of any other rough surfaces that stick together (burs and fur, Velcro fasteners). Encourage close observation while a feather edge is slowly pulled apart. Children should be able to see the hair-like barbs come apart.

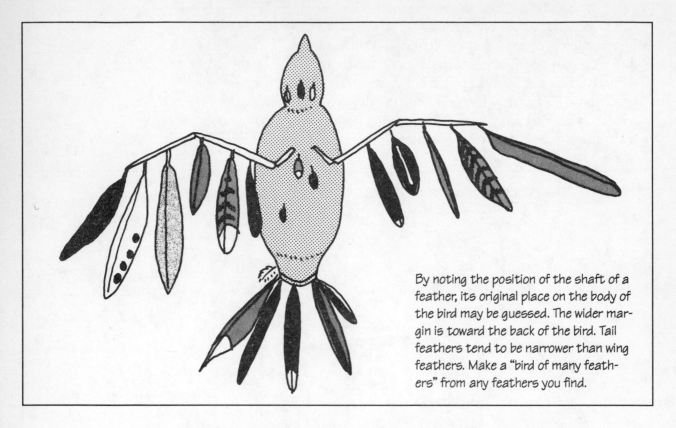

By noting the position of the shaft of a feather, its original place on the body of the bird may be guessed. The wider margin is toward the back of the bird. Tail feathers tend to be narrower than wing feathers. Make a "bird of many feathers" from any feathers you find.

■ Share these ideas for feather play or study. Encourage children to make up their own lists of activities to do with feathers.

- Tickle with it.

- Make a display of the three types of feathers: flight, body covering, and down.

- Find out where your skin is the most sensitive to touch; that is, discover the parts of your body where your skin has the most pressure-sensitive nerve endings. Do this activity by drawing a feather tip slowly over different sections of your face and hands.

- Imagine a story about a bird that dropped its feather. How did it feel to the bird to suddenly have the feather drop out?

- Use paint or ink to draw with a feather. Use both ends for different effects.

- If the feather is fluffy enough, blow it up in the air across the room. Try blowing it with your breath and fanning it with cardboard. Two or more children can have a feather race or play feather tennis.

Nests

Nest in Hand

Abandoned nests and molted feathers often give us our first tangible access to the lives of birds. The laws that forbid collection of currently used nests, viable eggs, and feathers are necessary restrictions. A collector's greed might easily diminish the number of birds in an area, and some of our rarest species are still threatened by the human desire to possess the precious. An abandoned nest, however, can stimulate questions and discussion about important aspects of bird life. Before proceeding with any activities involving a nest in hand, make sure the group understands that the nest was abandoned. Relate its history if you know it.

When a building is begun, large support structures are put in place first. Which parts of the nest look like these primary support structures? Some nests are made entirely of support structures. Ground nesters, such as killdeer and terns, and branch nesters, such as mourning doves, are among the species who build this sort of nest. With other birds, sides are built up on the nest using a secondary material like soft grasses and vines. A robin uses mud for this secondary material. A third layer, a soft lining of fine grass, hair, or fluffy material, may be used to line and insulate the nest.

Chipping sparrows make neat nests near the ends of long conifer branches. The preferred material for lining the nest cup is dark hair, sometimes taken right off the animal of choice. Nests have been found lined with silver Christmas tree tinsel.

TO DO

Without taking it apart, distinguish the different categories of materials used to create the nest. Make some guesses about which part of the nest took the most time to construct; estimate the relative amounts of each part to the whole (i.e., one-third small sticks, etc.).

Carefully dissect the nest. Sort the components according to size and function. Guess the size of a single beakful of each component and estimate the number of trips it would take to gather the material for the whole nest. If possible, find the outdoor source of each kind of material.

When humans try their hand at the nest-building process, the result is often a very inferior structure. Instead of duplicating the innate skills of birds, try to copy the process of nest building using comparable, human-made materials. Also, think about what a nest might look like if a bird had only human-made materials to work from, for example, junk from a landfill.

Nest in bird-selected site

It can be very difficult to tell if a nest is being used. In general, birds will build a new nest for each brood, but sometimes an old nest is in a choice site, and a new nest will be built over the old. Snooping humans can cause birds to desert a nest if the eggs haven't been laid yet or are newly laid. The safest rule is to stay away from nests in spring and summer.

There is still a great deal to be learned from a distance about nesting birds. Do both birds of the pair build the nest? Do special courtship gestures accompany the gathering of material or construction? How do the adult birds approach the nest? Do the birds share incubation duty? What is the timing of sitting and feeding breaks? Is food carried to the sitting bird? Are there more than two adult birds involved? How long does it take to build the

The nest of the northern oriole is made mostly of fibers of milkweed stalk, collected and woven by the female bird.

nest, incubate the eggs, and raise the nestling? What activities are special to each of those phases? What defense is taken against other birds and predators? If there is a second brood, are there any differences in the time needed to build the nest and raise the young?

TO DO

When the nest appears to be abandoned, have the children observe it at close range. (Leave the nest intact. The materials are likely to be recycled by other birds or remodeled and used by mice during the winter. In any case, it can be interesting to see which elements of the nest can last throughout the winter.) Ask the children to answer the following questions:

- How did the placement of the nest help to protect it?

- Is there any evidence of droppings in or around the nest?

- Can you see any remains of food?

- Are any infertile eggs or dead nestlings still present?

- If you can see into the nest, are there any parasites? (Your hand might attract some of them, noticeably the minute feather mites, they won't hurt you, but they will tickle as they swarm.)

Birds in Pictures and Stories: Owls

Owls are one of the most interesting bird families. They have all the wonderful avian attributes of feathered flight, keen eyesight and hearing, dramatic courtship, and the care of their young from egg to juvenile, but each aspect is special because of the owl's nocturnal life. Find out what the kids already know about owls. Ask how owls look different from other birds, what they eat, how they catch food, where they live, and what they sound like (have some fun with this last question—let each person be a calling owl). Accept all their information for now. If the statement is very far-fetched, perhaps respond with "I didn't know about that. We'll have to find out," just to place a question in the children's minds.

Once it has been established that owls eat smaller creatures, ask how an owl might find a mouse in the dark of night. Perhaps act out the scene. With eyes closed, have the children point in the direction of a noise you make with rustling papers or leaves. Owls are very good at locating prey by sounds. In tests, they have caught mice in completely darkened rooms. Other tests showed that some owls are very good at flying from perch to perch in the dark from memory.

TO DO

Do your own experiment with owl navigation. Lead a blindfolded child through a section of a room (from a chair to a door, for instance) several times. With help near at hand, let the "owl" try to walk the path alone. For

It may be easier to find an
owl at a museum or zoo
than to find one outdoors.

an owl, this ability to remember its home territory means that it can move
quickly to catch the rustling mouse without injuring itself.

The prey of the owl is not likely to know that the owl is approaching.
The soft quality of the owl's flight and body feathers eliminates any whoosh-
ing sound that might alert even a mouse. The act of catching is done by the
owl's strong toes, which are tipped with long, sharp claws called talons. The
talons both trap and kill the prey immediately.

The owl's hoot is well known, and the children can probably imitate
many versions of the sound. Although some of the smaller owls have voices
that sound more like a tremulous whistle, some of the larger owls have loud
hoots. Each species has a certain rhythm of hoots or wails to define its terri-

tory or call its mate. Owl families are likely to use a single "hoo-o" call to keep in touch with each other in the darkness. If possible, play some recordings of owl songs and let the children imitate the calls. A hoot will sound more

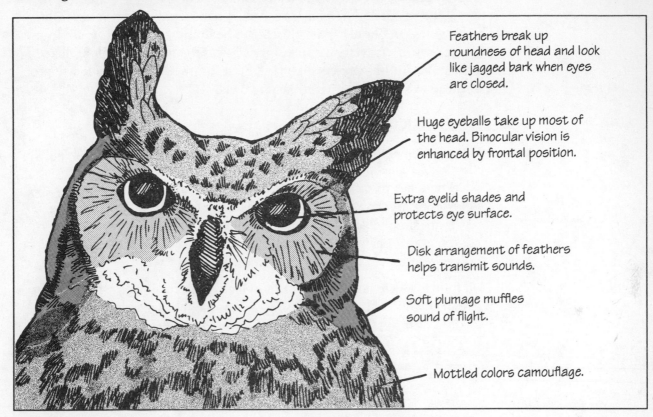

Feathers break up roundness of head and look like jagged bark when eyes are closed.

Huge eyeballs take up most of the head. Binocular vision is enhanced by frontal position.

Extra eyelid shades and protects eye surface.

Disk arrangement of feathers helps transmit sounds.

Soft plumage muffles sound of flight.

Mottled colors camouflage.

"owly" if the voice comes from the back of the throat and the air is pushed out by the abdominal muscles. Try out the hoots over a distance. Try out other birdlike calls to see which sounds carry best over distance. The deep resonance of an owl's call has excellent carrying power, especially at night.

The family life of an owl is different from the lives of most of our familiar songbirds. Great horned owls begin their courtship hooting in late winter. During this time the owls sing out their loudest and most rhythmic calls. Often the courtships involve operatic duets, with the male and female calling back and forth to each other.

When the bonding of the pair is completed, nesting and egg-laying begins. Unlike most songbirds, the first owl egg is incubated immediately and the embryo begins growth before a second egg is laid. This means that an owl family is somewhat like a human family, with offspring of several ages in the same nest. The strongest baby owls get the greatest share of the available food, and in seasons when prey populations are scarce, younger owls often starve and older ones survive. This natural sort of population control contributes to keeping the equation between predators and their food supply balanced.

The great horned owl is quite capable of seeing clearly during the daylight hours, but it is more effective at catching prey when it uses darkness to cover its hunting activities. Traits that enhance its hunting abilities are easy to see in any illustration.

TO DO

The owl's chunky body and front-facing eyes make them alluring subjects for craft projects. You will find many owls in books of art activities for children, but ask the children for ideas first. What shapes can be used for the body, wings, and head? What objects can be found around the house to use for the shapes? Two circular items placed near the top of an oblong shape seem sufficient to represent an owl. A hunt for owl shapes outside will probably lead to a wonderful assortment of owls.

TO THINK ABOUT

■ Superbly adapted for life in the dark, most owls are most active at night. Humans are adapted for life in the daylight, and our clumsiness during darkness has made us suspicious of the owls' "magical" abilities. Discuss movies or art showing owls. How are they represented? In most ways, owls are simply hawks that hunt at night, yet our culture views them as different from hawks and other birds of prey. Are there other nocturnal creatures that are seen as "spooky" or dangerous?

■ If humans were nocturnal animals, which diurnal animals might we fear as strangely different from us? Using owls as models, what adaptations would we need to make us successful as night beings?

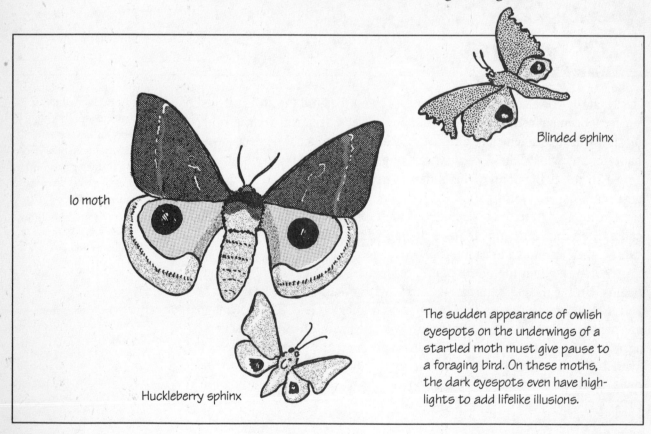

Blinded sphinx

Io moth

Huckleberry sphinx

The sudden appearance of owlish eyespots on the underwings of a startled moth must give pause to a foraging bird. On these moths, the dark eyespots even have highlights to add lifelike illusions.

First Birdwatching Experiences

Bird Walks without Birds

Sometimes you go outside to look for birds and there just aren't any to be found. In the middle of the day, the birds may be inactive. In wintertime, migratory birds may have left your area, and those that remain tend to flock together. In summer, birds with young will be watchful and quiet. But if you look carefully, there will still be evidence of birds. To find birds, search for the items described in this section. As you spend time watching birds go about their business, you will be able to add more birding opportunities of your own.

Nests

Children are great at finding nests. Kids can get under shrubs and look up through the branches—the best technique for spotting the bristly outline of a nest. At first you may only spot the more obvious nests of squirrels. Squirrel nests are bigger than most songbird nests and more rounded on the tops. Grey and fox squirrel nests are near large branches (as are the nests of crows and jays, but the bird nests are flatter and twiggier). Red squirrel nests are most likely to be dense globes of leaves out on the thin upper branches of trees. Hawks and owls build nests larger than both those mentioned above.

Important: *It is against the law to gather nests. At one time nest collecting was a major hobby. Laws to prevent commercial exploitation of birds have since been enacted. Even though most songbirds use their nests only one time, a child's enthusiasm may lead to the destruction of a nest during breeding season. It is essential that respect for the bird's "property" be demonstrated to children.*

You can still learn a great deal without destroying the nest. Try to figure out why the birds chose that site for a nest. Where was the material collected? How could the bird get the material without tools or great strength? Are the materials the same inside the nest as outside? Which material was brought in first? Go on a "nesting hunt" and try to find the same materials in the area. You might even try to build a nest.

Droppings

Though not the most glamorous evidence of bird life, feces are a definite indication that birds are nearby. Don't hesitate to point out droppings to children. They may make a lot of noise about it, but they will be interested. Use words for feces that they know.

Bird droppings are a combination of both urine and feces. Their lack of identifiable waste products is the result of a highly efficient, high-powered metabolism. Although you probably won't be able to identify the bird by its droppings, there are some questions to ask and information to be found. Do you think the bird was big or little? Do you think the perch was used often? (Are there lots of droppings?) Look for feathers also. A hawk or owl might have plucked its prey on the spot. If the droppings seem to be dense enough to be picked up and carried, they might be from baby birds, deposited some distance from the nest by the parent bird. How could evidence such as droppings near the nest endanger the babies? (Some predators would soon learn that a concentration of droppings means lunch is nearby.)

Some fruit seeds will pass through a bird's digestive system whole and ready to grow. Very often the berry bushes found growing along a fence row or under an overhead wire are direct results of those once-eaten seeds. Check the fruit of plants in those areas. Look for berries that are bright when ripe (or dark and shiny like a bird's eye) and easy to pluck. Many bird-berry plants drop their fruits when ripe, perhaps giving mice chances at moving the seeds.

Pellets

Some parts of the food birds eat are regurgitated and dropped as pellets. Most birds would be weighed down by a stomachful of indigestibles such as large seeds or prey parts (hair, feathers, or bones). After being sorted out from food substances in the gizzard, the indigestibles are gathered into a compacted cylindrical object called a pellet. The pellet is held for a time in the throat area, then coughed up and out. Probably all birds produce pellets

Owl pellets are practically "dry cleaned" packages of the fur and bones of their prey. Inside the tightly packed fur are the tiny bones of mammals, birds, or small reptiles.

(or "cough balls"), but the larger products of hawks, owls, and other predators are the most likely to be found. The discovery of a pellet indicates that a roosting place may be overhead, and also may lead to a discovery of what the bird has been eating. For biologists, the study of bird pellets can show the seasonal changes of diet and the availability of prey, as well as changes in the general environment. For the curious naturalist, the contents of a dissected owl pellet can bring the life of the elusive bird up close.

Children may be hesitant to handle an owl pellet. Although it looks as though it might smell bad, the material has been thoroughly "dry cleaned" by the digestive juices of the gizzard, so there is little odor and nothing slimy. Dissecting tools or two forks or toothpicks work well to help you and the children examine the pellet. As it is pulled apart, small bones, teeth, or skulls can be seen within the matting of fur or feathers. Field guides to mammals often have illustrations of identified skulls, but just the process of sorting the material and estimating the number and size of prey can give the group some idea of what owls eat.

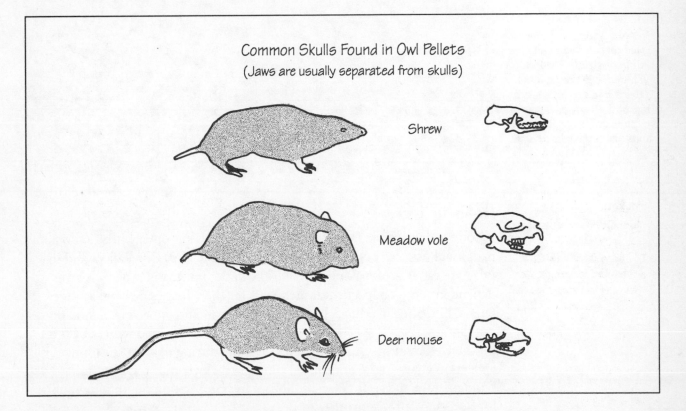

Common Skulls Found in Owl Pellets
(Jaws are usually separated from skulls)

Shrew

Meadow vole

Deer mouse

The children might think the process of coughing up wads of fur is a bother to a bird, but it is actually necessary to its health. It is known, for instance, that the health of caged hawks and owls suffers if they are fed only raw skinless meat. The addition of feltlike wrapping to take the place of fur or feathers and the subsequent creation of pellets assures the birds' health. The reason for this is not certain. Perhaps the feltlike material protects the digestive tract from sharp bones. Can the children think of any other reasons the pellets are healthful?

Bird tracks in wet sand or mud present some clues for the birder-sleuth. The lack of a hind toe in the print indicates a wading, not a perching, bird. The two lengths of toes and stride give some hints about the relative sizes of the two birds.

Holes in Trees

Woodpeckers are the main creators of tree holes, but other birds (and mammals) will use tree cavities as nesting or roosting sites. Chickadees and titmice are capable of making holes in soft wood, but many other birds are dependent on woodpeckers as architects for their homes. Several kinds of wrens, bluebirds, starlings, house sparrows, tree and violet-green swallows, nuthatches, several species of owls, American kestrels, and wood ducks all nest in tree cavities. Quiet watching of a hole during nesting season may give good views of the birds listed above or the original woodpecker builders. (See the section on birdhouses for information on building homes for birds in your own yard.)

Counting Local Birds

No one can know exactly how many birds are in any given area. The changes in both numbers and species of total populations can be estimated by recording just small numbers of birds at one place over a length of time.

For instance, a chart that shows the numbers and varieties of birds seen on the way to school each morning throughout the school year can give information on the movements of migratory birds and the stability of local bird populations. If other conditions are also recorded, the effects of weather, breeding seasons, and changes in the food supplies may also be discussed.

The area of observation need not be extensive, the number of birds may be small, and the period of time spent observing may be short. If the count is made on a regular basis (and the count is accurate), interesting patterns in the lives of birds can be seen. The following opportunities can be used for counting birds on a regular basis:

- Commutes that occur daily, weekly, or monthly

- Frequent walks through the same area

- Observation periods at a feeding station

- Lunch hours at a park.

Measuring the Fright Distances of Various Birds

Beginning birders are often frustrated when birds fly away as they are aproached for closer observation. The following activity turns that interaction into a learning experience. Different species of birds have different tolerances of people. Chickadees are known for their fearlessness, but mourning doves are likely to flutter off at the least movement.

The experiment is to find out if different species have consistently different fright distances. The procedure is to approach a bird until it takes off. One marker is dropped at the spot where the observer is standing when the bird takes flight; a second marker is dropped at the spot where the bird leaves the ground. The distance between the markers is recorded. The procedure must be repeated a number of times, using at least two species of birds for comparison. Discuss the following considerations with the participants:

- *The markers*. They must fall straight down and stand out clearly from a distance. Pencils, wads of paper, or pieces of cloth are good choices.

- *The unit of measure*. A long tape measure would be helpful, but other units such as shoe lengths or stride lengths may be handier and can be converted to yards or meters later.

- *The speeds of approach*. Results will be affected by the speed of your approach. A fast approach will produce longer fright distances. Decide on your approach speed before you begin. Practice it. (If you only have one species of bird to observe, the effect of different speeds might be your experiment.)

- *The recording method*. Set up a worksheet that includes the species of bird, what the bird was doing when observed, your speed of approach, the fright distance, the time of year (breeding birds might react differently from winter flocks), and any other observations.

■ *The species of birds to be observed.* Ground-feeding birds will give the clearest results. Pigeons, starlings, sparrows, robins, gulls, and doves are all good subjects. Seed can be put out to attract the birds, or an established backyard feeder can be used.

■ *The number of times each species should be tested.* Try to convey the idea that the more times the procedure is repeated, the greater the chance of correctly predicting a result or drawing a conclusion. You know your group's tolerance, however. The main goal should be to cultivate an interest in observing birds.

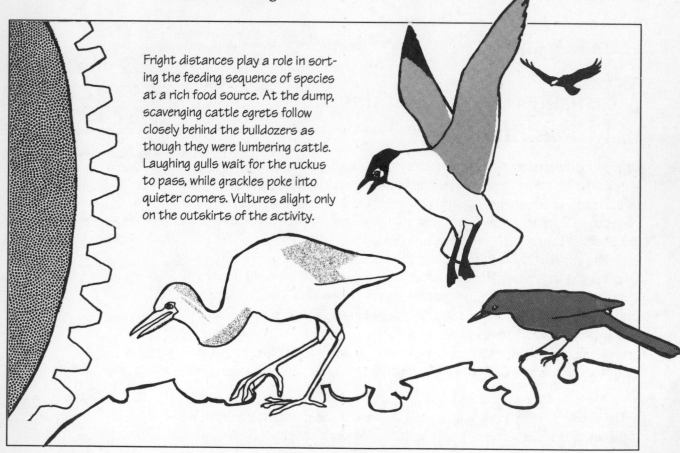

Fright distances play a role in sorting the feeding sequence of species at a rich food source. At the dump, scavenging cattle egrets follow closely behind the bulldozers as though they were lumbering cattle. Laughing gulls wait for the ruckus to pass, while grackles poke into quieter corners. Vultures alight only on the outskirts of the activity.

When all the data has been gathered, discuss the results as a group. Get some sense of the correlation between fright distance and species from the measurements and other observations. This is a great opportunity to use math skills. The fright distances of each species can be averaged, expressed as a range (shortest to longest), plotted on a graph, or translated into smaller units on strips of paper or with stickers on construction paper. Think of ways to express the data visually.

TO WATCH FOR

Look for unusually tame behavior, such as very short fright distance, in free-living birds. Relative lack of fear in birds occurs when (1) birds associate people with food (parks, farms, outdoor restaurants) or (2) birds don't ever see people (Arctic birds such as snowy owls).

How to Use Binoculars

For beginning birders of any age, first attempts to use binoculars can be frustrating. A bird that is easily seen with the naked eye can take long moments to relocate through field glasses, usually just as long as it takes for the bird to fly away. Only repeated practice makes the process easy.

Finding a moving bird without binoculars isn't very difficult; the human brain naturally picks up on small movements in the field of vision. Once the bird is spotted, however, the watcher's eyes must hold their position while the binoculars are raised and focused. If the eyes (or the bird) move, don't search with the binoculars. It is always faster to take the glasses down, relocate the bird, and try again.

Practicing with mock binoculars helps to train the eye muscles. Use two paper tubes (toilet tissue tubes are ideal) or make double circles with fingers and thumbs as if holding up invisible binoculars. Practice on a near object at first. Spot it, then sight it again through the mock binocs. Distant objects are slightly more difficult to relocate, as are small birds. Practice the process of spot and resight until that part of birdwatching becomes second nature.

Birding with a Group:
Helping Each Other Find Birds

Birdwatching with others provides opportunities to see more birds and more bird behaviors. A group of birders can discover birds in different directions and can note more attributes of a single bird. It helps to decide ahead of time which participants will watch for each attribute. The manner of flying, colors of feathers, shapes of wings and tail, distinctive markings, size, and sounds are categories that can be assigned to individuals or teams within the group. Pencils, clip boards, and lists of common bird attributes can help you gather data and focus attention. Identifications can then be made by pooling the data and discussing possibilities.

It may not always be easy for everyone to find a particular bird at the same time. Yelling out for everyone to look and pointing with an extended arm toward the bird is a good way to make a bird disappear. Good birding technique requires low voices (no hissing whispers) and no abrupt gestures or pointing. Among some Native American peoples, pointing with a thrust of a chin is considered sufficient. Perhaps this evolved as a hunter's gesture. See if it works in your group.

Focusing the group's attention on a small bird in a large landscape is a challenge made easier by transposing the face of a clock on the area being observed. If the group is looking for a bird in a tree, for instance, the top of the tree would be twelve o'clock, the far right, three o'clock, the base, six, and the far left, nine o'clock. If the bird is closer to the center, give an approximate position relative to the center and its nearest clock position ("Warbler left of center, about ten o'clock").

If you are looking for birds in an open field or over water, impose the clock face on the encircling horizon before you begin. Choose a distinct landmark as twelve o'clock and agree on the positions of three, six, and nine o'clock also. The short time it takes to set up your "mapping system" contributes greatly to the group's full participation. In the open, you are likely to be viewing moving birds, so include directional information ("Ducks at three o'clock, moving left").

 ## TO WATCH FOR

When observing birds in an open area, try to figure out where birds are flying *to*. Is there a food source nearby? Are they influenced by wind direction? Are they migrating?

PART THREE

BIRD BODIES

The activities in this section are about human anatomy and life cycles. Frankly, the use of birds to illustrate the lessons is a ploy. I found when I was teaching biology to children that the best way to get them thinking about their own bodies was to use a snake (a six-foot boa) to talk about body parts and their functions. Never mind that the snake didn't have arms, legs, eyelids, external ears, hair, or molars. Getting the kids to think about how the snake managed to live without all those valuable body parts made it easier to learn about the lives of both snakes and children. It's an interesting concept: we seem to learn best by comparison and by being challenged by apparent weirdness.

"Teaching with Strangeness" is best done as a symmetrical process. Show the kids something wonderful about birds that catches their attention, contrast it with something ordinary about their own lives that they may not have thought about, and ask them to use the idea and their imagination to create a new "creature." For example, ask the children how their arm structure is like that of a bird. Then, ask them to use that information to draw their own arm as a bird wing. The wing will be based on real structures, but the expression will be individual, unique to the creator.

Learning about the early lives of other life forms is crucial to children. They find out about young birds and they find out about themselves. It gives them a chance to ask questions about their bodies and a vocabulary for doing so. It helps to know that other life forms find it difficult to be young and vulnerable, and it helps to learn that innate strengths and abilities will help them through their early lives. Our minds can make powerful use of analogies. By listening to children's stories and looking at their drawings, you may come across self-expressions that indicate fears or needs. You may find that discussions of resolutions to the bird's problems gives children the means of solving their own problems.

TO DO

Have each child make a drawing of a soaring bird. (The drawings can be kept private or they can be shared with the group.) The bird's story will come to each child as he or she works. Ask the children: What do you find of your own story in your drawing? How does the drawing make you feel?

Early Life:
Eggs and Babies

The Egg

It really is a remarkable process: a developing individual is encased in a membrane that is thin enough to let gases through, yet thick enough to protect the young creature from attack by smaller organisms. Food is stored inside the membrane so that the embryonic animal can grow. By the time hatching occurs, the young animal is able to interact with its environment well enough to feed itself or elicit food from its parents. Life begins in an egg for a wide variety of animals. Butterflies, snails, sharks, goldfish, lobsters, earthworms, spiders, turtles, some snakes, fish, toads, alligators, salamanders, lizards, honeybees, platypi, and all birds leave their mothers' bodies as eggs. Although many other kinds of animals tend their eggs in various ways, usually just protecting them from predation, birds use their body warmth to sustain the life

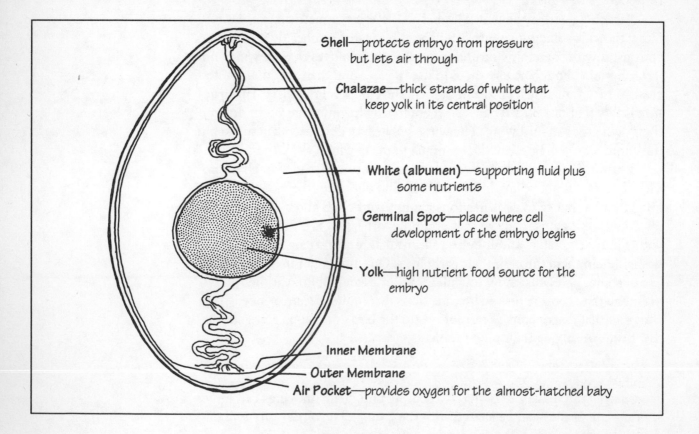

Shell—protects embryo from pressure but lets air through

Chalazae—thick strands of white that keep yolk in its central position

White (albumen)—supporting fluid plus some nutrients

Germinal Spot—place where cell development of the embryo begins

Yolk—high nutrient food source for the embryo

Inner Membrane

Outer Membrane

Air Pocket—provides oxygen for the almost-hatched baby

inside. Without that warmth, the embryo will die. Perhaps the most appropriate egg analogy is a space capsule. To live and grow, the creature inside the eggshell must have supplies of air and food as well as warmth and protection from an overwhelmingly dangerous environment. Until it can develop defenses and begin to learn appropriate behaviors, it stays inside.

TO DO

- Make as complete a list as possible of animals other than birds that lay eggs. Try to include only the eggs that the group has seen or touched so that their attributes and environments can be described from experience. Discuss textures, colors, size, and place of discovery. Try to identify the attributes that make them all eggs; see if you can list those attributes that differ from the eggs of birds.

- Try to take apart a bird egg. Use hard-boiled chicken eggs, one for each person. Ask for descriptions of the surface of the shell. A magnifying glass will show the tiny holes that let oxygen in and carbon dioxide out. Water vapor can also leave the egg through these pores. In incubators, the moisture in the air must be kept high to keep the eggs from drying out.

- Try rolling an egg in a straight line. The pear shape causes the egg to roll in a curve. The eggs of cliff-nesting seabirds are even more pointed at one end, making them less likely to roll over the edge of the bird's habitat.

- Despite its fragility, the eggshell can take a surprising amount of pressure. Using an uncooked egg, squeeze the egg in one hand, pressing against the pointed ends rather than the sides. (The egg will break eventually, so be prepared for a mess. A broken raw egg could be used for identification of parts.)

- Open a hard-boiled egg by gently cracking the side against a hard surface, then roll it between two hands to fracture the whole surface. Taking off the shell piece by piece can be frustrating when you're hungry, but enlightening when considering the toughness and integrity of the membrane that lies between the shell and the white. There are actually two membranes, one inside the other. They separate at the wide end to form an air space. The air that collects in this space keeps the ready-to-hatch baby alive until it can scrape an opening in the shell.

- The inner membrane encloses the fluids of the liquid white. To this inner membrane flexible strands attach, holding the yolk suspended so that the embryo develops on the upper side of the yolk in the approximate center of the egg. Cooking will destroy the strands, but the yolk of a boiled egg, if freshly laid, will always be in the same position because of them.

- The yolk contains both the ovum (the cell capable of growing into a bird) and its food supply. Once fertilized, the ovum (identifiable as a germinal spot of red on a fresh yolk) begins to use the food supply to power the increasingly complicated growth of the forming embryo. As the chick grows larger, the yolk and the white, also a source of nourishment, shrink.

■ Spin both a raw and a boiled egg. The boiled egg will spin for much longer. In a raw egg, the movement of the fluid whites and the stretchiness of the supporting membranes mean that the denser yolk moves out of the center. As when a rapidly spinning ice skater extends her arms, the weight of the off-center yolk slows the spin to a stop.

How an Egg Is Made

The journey made by an egg through the mother bird begins with a shell-less unfertilized ovum. At the time of ripeness, the one-celled ovum and its food supply, the yolk, begin to move down the reproductive tube. As the ovum travels, it is provided with additional layers of nutrients and protection. The layers of clear egg "white" form first, followed by the formation of the shell just before it leaves the parent. In most birds the whole process takes about twenty-four hours.

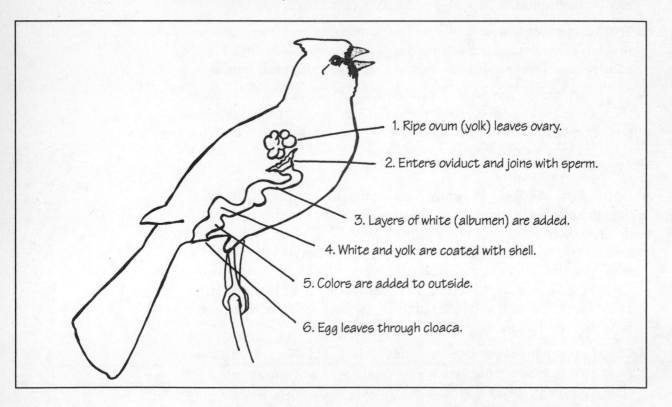

1. Ripe ovum (yolk) leaves ovary.

2. Enters oviduct and joins with sperm.

3. Layers of white (albumen) are added.

4. White and yolk are coated with shell.

5. Colors are added to outside.

6. Egg leaves through cloaca.

Each step of the journey is important to the development of a baby bird. In the first step, the round yolk and ovum separate from the ovary and begin to travel down the *oviduct,* or egg tube. If sperm are present, fertilization takes place at this time. Fertilization is not necessary in the formation process, but growth of a baby bird will not occur without it.

As the egg descends, layers of *albumen* are secreted by the walls of the oviduct. The first layer and its supportive chords are denser than the white and can be seen in raw eggs as the membrane surrounding the yolk and twisted, whitish strands attached on either side. The strands, called *chalazae,* serve to suspend the yolk near the center of the egg. The yolk nutrients are denser than the undeveloped embryo cells. In its journey down the oviduct, the "ballast" of the heavier yolk nutrients holds the yolk steady as the egg white and shell rotate around it, twisting the chalazae.

Two other membranes enclose the yolk and its white before the shell covering is secreted by the oviduct walls. The inner layer surrounds the white, and the outer layer adheres to the shell. They separate at the air space at the wider point of the shell and can be best observed in a boiled chicken egg. Colors may be mixed in with the whitish calcium matrix of the shell, and they may be applied in a separate operation. Dark streaks or wiggly splotches of color are the result of the oviduct's "hiccuping" as the pigment squirts from pores surrounding the egg.

The egg is laid soon after the shell is formed, but most birds prefer a morning time for laying. Wild-living birds only lay their eggs in nests (not necessarily their own). The nest itself seems to be a stimulus to laying, although many birds do seem able to "count," since each species usually lays a particular number of eggs. Ducks, geese, and chicken-like birds lay the largest number of eggs, while one egg is typical of many oceangoing seabirds. Most songbirds lay three to six eggs; the littlest ones (wrens, kinglets, and chickadees) can lay up to eight. During the period of laying, some birds can be induced to lay many more than the usual number if eggs are taken from the nest. This experiment was tried with a northern flicker, who responded by replacing her kidnapped eggs seventy-one times (before the experimenter stopped).

TO DO

■ Although the father and mother birds must keep their eggs covered for protection and warmth, the eggs are sometimes left exposed. If the eggs are easy to see, they are likely to be eaten. Protective coloration, shape-hiding colors, and splotches minimize the losses. You can make a game of "evolving" protective coloration on eggs so that they are camouflaged to match a familiar area. Use acrylic paints (watercolors won't stick), gummed stickers, and/or glued-on paper, fabric, or actual bits of the habitat. Have several boiled eggs for each participant so that different ideas can be tried. When the camouflaged eggs are finished, test them in the field with an egg hunt. The hiders then become the hunters, and the hidden eggs are collected. You may choose to ask the children to write down the location of each egg to give every hunter a chance to find several eggs. After a time of hunting, go around as a group to collect the eggs, giving each child a chance to explain his or her hiding techniques.

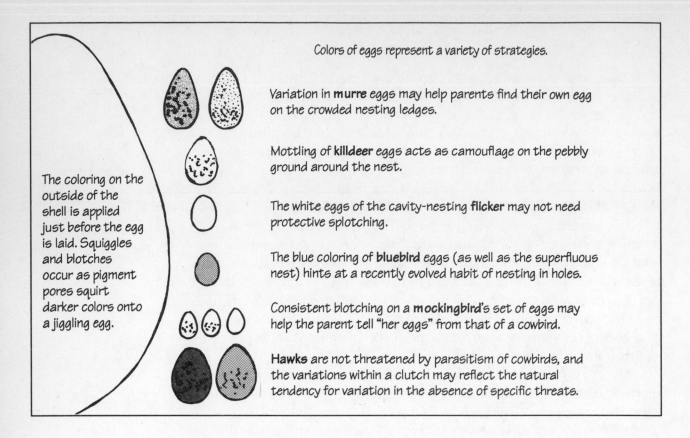

Colors of eggs represent a variety of strategies.

Variation in **murre** eggs may help parents find their own egg on the crowded nesting ledges.

Mottling of **killdeer** eggs acts as camouflage on the pebbly ground around the nest.

The white eggs of the cavity-nesting **flicker** may not need protective splotching.

The blue coloring of **bluebird** eggs (as well as the superfluous nest) hints at a recently evolved habit of nesting in holes.

Consistent blotching on a **mockingbird's** set of eggs may help the parent tell "her eggs" from that of a cowbird.

Hawks are not threatened by parasitism of cowbirds, and the variations within a clutch may reflect the natural tendency for variation in the absence of specific threats.

The coloring on the outside of the shell is applied just before the egg is laid. Squiggles and blotches occur as pigment pores squirt darker colors onto a jiggling egg.

- Mimic the process of evolution by having a subsequent camouflaging session using only the colorings of the eggs that were found less often. In nature, the eggs found less often would be most likely to hatch. Have another hunt to see how well the players can find this second group of eggs.

- You may find that the hunters have improved their egg-finding techniques as well, a problem for prey species in nature as well.

The Baby Bird—Just Out of the Egg

The newly hatched young bird looks very different from the parent who cares for it—except, that is, for its big feet. Within several days a young bird's feet will be as large as its parents' feet. The rest of the baby, however, will still go through many changes before it can take care of itself. For most birds this growth happens in a very short time: less than a month from hatchling to young adult. Most songbirds will be parents themselves the following spring. Ask the children what baby birds they have seen. Talk about what the babies looked like and how they acted.

Hatchlings That Are Helpless

Some babies, including the offspring of common songbirds, are hatched while still in an immature and dependent condition. These altricial young have only a few fluffy feathers on their bodies. Their eyes are closed, and their bodies are very weak. When they feel a parent bird nearby, they stretch out their necks and open their large mouths wide. The inside of their mouths is brightly colored in reds or yellows, so that the parent arriving

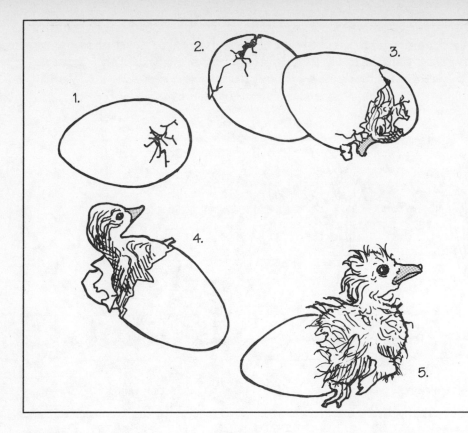

The hatching process (pipping) may take a day to achieve. The cramped hatchling must first crack the shell to create a circular opening, then force the shell apart. The only tool available is the "egg tooth," a sharp projection on the end of the beak.

with food looks down at several gaping targets. The baby that makes the most noise gets the most food poked down its throat. When the parents can find sufficient food, all the young survive. If food is scarce, the weakest young grow more slowly and may die. By feeding the most vigorous babies first, the parents are more likely to have some offspring reach maturity despite poor conditions. (Young children may be worried by this seemingly heartless behavior of the parent birds. It may help to tell them that the parents are led by their instinct to push food into the liveliest mouth. Bird lives are so difficult that only the healthiest birds can live. Human instincts are different. In human families the parents strive to care for each child, regardless of their weaknesses.)

Exactly when a young altricial bird leaves its nest depends often on where the nest is built. For the young of several species of ground-nesting warblers, the nest is deserted within one week, even though the babies can't fully fly. Young robins or cardinals may leave their nests in trees or shrubs after two weeks and fly several days after that. Woodpecker young, safer in their cavity nests, may stay put for a month, then fly well on the first try.

Within a couple of weeks after hatching, songbird babies have grown as large as their parents. A full set of feathers cover the body and form wings and a tail. Usually the feathers are not as brightly colored as those of the parent birds; the camouflage offers extra protection for the young bird, who is not so skilled at hunting and hiding. If the young songbird is a migratory bird, it will begin to move south, often in a group with its same species or a mixture of other species. If the birds are local year-round species, they will usually flock with others of their kind. Large flocks of crows, starlings, and mourning doves are seen at this time. Smaller birds may make mixed flocks.

Most nestlings hatch at the same time and grow up together. Quail chicks hatch out all together and leave their nest to follow their mother shortly after hatching. Owls, hawks, and herons hatch out of their eggs on successive days, in the order they were laid. If the prey is scarce, only the stronger oldest survive.

Barn owls

Bob-white

Chickadees, nuthatches, and woodpeckers or juncos and various sparrows may form flocks for the winter months.

Hatchlings That Are Strong

Some children may have seen the down-covered hatchlings of ducks and chickens. These strong and independent precocial young have a different life story. They spend a longer time growing inside their eggs. The eggs are larger and contain more food for their developing embryos. Shortly after hatching from their eggs, ducklings or chicks are wide-eyed and alert. Their bodies are covered with short, fluffy feathers, and they can walk about within a very short time. The young birds have an instinctive urge to peck at foodlike items, and after several days of pecking and observing the eating habits of adults, they are able to feed themselves.

The next stage varies with the species of bird. Young sandpipers and plovers, for instance, are on their own soon after birth. The adults fly south from the Arctic breeding grounds, and the young feed themselves on the abundant insect life, migrating a short time later using instinctual instructions. Geese, ducks, turkeys, quail, and grouse stay together in family groups, joining flocks for the winter months, then separating for the summer breeding season.

The young of some species have qualities of both altricial and precocial birds. Young hawks, owls, vultures, herons, and gulls are born with a downy covering but are dependent on their parents for food. The length of their dependency varies with the species, but in general, the larger the bird, the longer the time it lives in the nest.

Counting from the day the eggs were laid, both these baby birds are about a month old. The killdeer chick was just hatched, however. Similar to other precocial young, in one day it can run about, regulate its own body temperature, and find its food. The altricial wren chick hatched out nearly featherless and has been cared for by its parents for two weeks. It is now able to move about and is experimenting with finding its own food.

Killdeer

House wren

TO DO

Have each child choose a kind of bird to be, using his or her name as the species name (i.e., Molly Duck, Fred Hawk, or Jessica Swallow). Using the life histories of actual birds for reference, illustrate and describe the general characteristics of the three life stages: (1) "When I was an egg I looked like this"; (2) "When I was a hatchling I looked like this, I lived (where), and I got my food (how)"; and (3) "As an adult I looked like this and found my food (how) and (where)." Since the birds are imaginary, the children do not have to stick strictly to reality, but the stages should reflect an understanding of the basic differences between dependent-born (altricial) and ready-to-go (precocial) hatchlings.

Which Came First: The Chicken or the Egg?

This old riddle has no correct answers, but discussing the possibilities can bring out some interesting issues and help clarify notions of bird life cycles. Your discussion will also provide a good lesson in the scientific process of asking a good question in order to get a good answer. The questions How does a chicken begin? and Where does an egg come from? will lead the children to a discussion of bird reproduction. Ask the children what they think and why.

Some reptiles and all birds start their lives encased in protective shells.

The best defense for babies that leave their nest immediately after hatching is to hold still. This wild baby turkey is relying on its very good camouflage to hide it from predators.

Although a turtle and a turkey look very different from each other, there are shared characteristics such as scaly feet and the way the skull bones fit together. In the same way, two cousins may have similar-looking eyes and find that their mutual grandmother had the same shape to her eyes.

Fossil imprints of long-ago creatures have features of both reptiles and birds. Rock that was once soft mud holds images of animals with lizardy teeth and feathered arms. Perhaps they could only glide from tree to tree, but those gliders that could sail farther must have stood a better chance of surviving and producing more offspring. Over millions of generations, millions of successes and deaths, the characteristics of modern bird species evolved. Those species that produced the most varied offspring with the greatest adaptability lasted over the longest time. It would seem that, for the creation of a new bird species, the eggs must come first. The varied young that hatch from them will carry the heritage of the species and adapt to the world's changes.

When members of a species become separated from others of their species, this "law of variability" can result in large-scale changes in shape or color so that the separate groups no longer resemble each other.

Some birds once thought to be separate species have recently been found to be able to breed with each other and produce fertile offspring (separate species cannot produce fertile offspring). Older bird books name an eastern oriole "the Baltimore oriole" and a western oriole "the Bullock's oriole." Now recognized as the same species, they have both been renamed the northern oriole. Separated by huge tracts of habitat unsuitable for orioles, the once-similar population of birds have gradually evolved superficial dif-

A close-up view of any bird (in this case, a brown thrasher) shows some features that still look vaguely reptilian.

ferences. Their plumage patterns and song patterns are not the same, but where their ranges overlap, superficially different individuals recognize each other as mates and breed fertile young.

The apparent differences in the orioles are the result of random changes. Every new generation of birds must overcome predators, poor weather conditions, and limited food supplies. The individuals that succeed against those odds and mate successfully will produce another generation. Those birds facing the same problems as their parents are more likely to survive if they resemble their parents. If the environment is changing, however, different bodies and behaviors give the best survival value.

TO DO

The children can experience the interaction of bird, habitat, and the process of natural selection by playing a hunting game with jelly beans as the prey. Start with a known number of jelly beans, with equal numbers of each color. The beans are the Multicolored Jelly Birds, a species much hunted by fierce, sweet-toothed Sharp-eyed Jellyeaters. Scatter the Jelly Birds over a limited area that has a predominant color matching at least one bean color (lawn, carpet, etc.). Explain to the Jellyeaters that they have thirty seconds to catch (but not eat) all the Jelly Birds they can find. Have the children tally their catches by color. Figure out which color of Jelly Birds will have the greatest chance of living to produce offspring. Try the game again in a differently colored environment and check results. If the Jellybirds migrated to a different habitat or could live in a variety of habitats, or if the background changed with the seasons, a variety of colorations would benefit the entire population. In fact, this is just what occurs in nature.

TO THINK ABOUT

Discuss the lives of the most common birds in your area and try to figure out the adaptations (colors, shapes, habits, or foods) that allow the birds to reproduce successfully. In many cases, a large and variable range of adaptations, rather than a limiting specialization, makes for survival.

TO WATCH FOR

Look for color variations in flocks of birds. Unusual white feathers are easiest to spot, but look for darker (melanistic) feathers, as well.

Adult Parts and Adaptations

Anatomy Lessons from the Grocery Store: The Chicken

The inner structures of most birds are inaccessible to our experience, but the chicken of the meat department can illustrate many of the physical features found in all birds. Perhaps even more interesting to a child, discussion of a bird's body provides an opportunity to learn about one's own body.

Use an uncooked fryer for your discussion of the outside of a bird; it's flexible and recognizable as a creature. Even without its feet and head, the whole fryer can show the following features, some or all of which can be investigated at one time:

- Parts analogous to human body parts
- Adaptations for flying (fewer bones than land animals, hollow bones, large flight muscles, streamlined torso)
- Attachment of the feathers to the skin
- The neck, various organs, and glands.

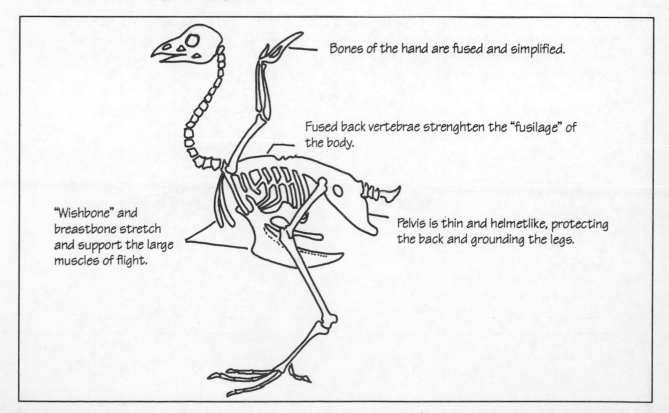

Bones of the hand are fused and simplified.

Fused back vertebrae strenghten the "fusilage" of the body.

"Wishbone" and breastbone stretch and support the large muscles of flight.

Pelvis is thin and helmetlike, protecting the back and grounding the legs.

Note: Some children may never have confronted the idea that some of their food comes off an animal's body. Since the goal is to make the connection that the chicken was once a live bird, be sensitive to the children's revulsion or even queasiness. Try to be straightforward as you handle the chicken. Rough or finicky gestures will be emotionally distracting and prevent the children from appreciating the experience. If someone does feel overwhelmed, suggest that he or she take a break such as a walk or another activity. Stepping away for a minute gives a person a chance to adjust to the sight and the new awareness.

Muscles

The flight muscles of the breast and the walking muscles of the legs can be seen and felt. The difference between large muscles and bony areas can be easily distinguished by squeezing or pressing with fingers. (Note: Be sure hands and the chicken are thoroughly washed; salmonella contamination is common on raw poultry.) Encourage the children to identify similar muscle groups on their bodies.

The human muscles similar to those used by birds for flight can be experienced by the children on their own bodies after even sixty seconds of imitating the back-to-front flapping action of a flying bird. Point out the greater muscle size in the chicken breast (downstroke) muscles compared with the smaller back (upstroke) muscles. Ask the children why that might be. The experience of climbing stairs might be compared to flying: the pushing-down muscles must work more than the lifting-up muscles for both actions.

The inside of the upper arm bone of a chicken (the "drumstick" of the wing) shows two special attributes of bird bones. Many bird bones are hollow (tubes are stronger than slabs) with branching inner reinforcements, like struts on a bridge. On most birds, this bone also contains a balloonlike air sac, part of the system that ventilates and cools the flying bird.

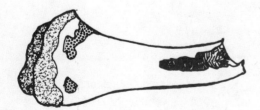

Limbs

Show that the chicken can "stand up" and resemble a (headless) person. Begin your examination of the limbs by looking carefully at the chicken's "hands." The thumb bone can be distinguished sticking out in front of the wrist joint. The rest of the fingers seem to be melted together but are actually simplified so that only one finger supports the entire "hand" of the wing. Find the elbow of the wing and the two bones of the lower arm. Have the children feel them and compare them with the pair of bones in their own arms.

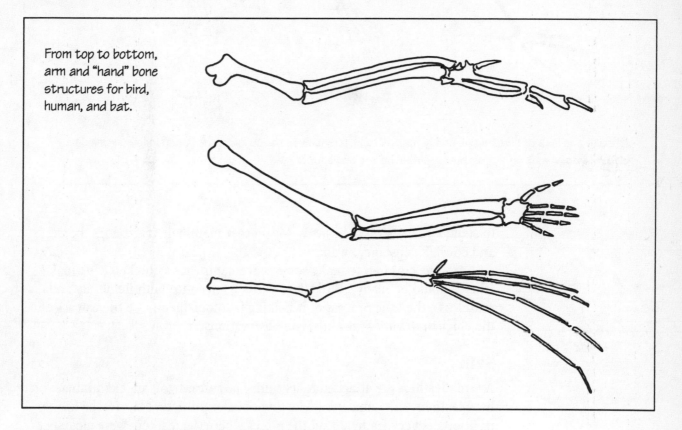

From top to bottom, arm and "hand" bone structures for bird, human, and bat.

Challenge the children to try to position their arms and legs to look like birds. This is silly enough to be a lot of fun.

Birds' legs are a little harder to compare to human legs. The part we tend to think of as the bird's foot is really its toes; one or two toes point backward to stabilize the bird in walking or to help the bird grasp its perch or prey. A bird is on tiptoe all the time. The rest of the foot is the scaly section above the toes. The feathers begin at the ankle joint, covering the drumstick, or lower leg. Above the knee, the short thigh connects to the hip joint. After the children attempt to stand like birds, discuss how this seemingly uncomfortable tiptoe position might be an advantage in jumping, running, and landing. If possible, look at pictures that show the legs of other animals. Humans, bears, and raccoons are the only North American animals

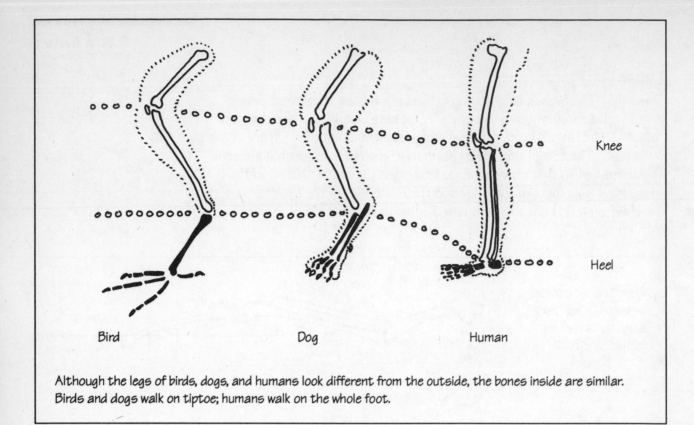

Knee

Heel

Bird　　　　　　　Dog　　　　　　　Human

Although the legs of birds, dogs, and humans look different from the outside, the bones inside are similar. Birds and dogs walk on tiptoe; humans walk on the whole foot.

to stand and walk on their heels. Most other mammals (cats, dogs, horses, and cows, for instance) walk on tiptoe.

Ask the children to make some movements that a chicken can't make (there should be many). Birds have partially given up both flexibility and muscles in the long process of becoming fabulous fliers. Use the carcass of the chicken to verify the children's observations.

Skin

A bird's feathers are attached to its skin. The carcass you are examining won't have feathers, but you can see the tiny hole, or pore, that marks the former position of every feather. Find the places where the feathers were closest together. Find any areas where there were no feathers. The largest pores are attachments for the large wing and tail feathers. The wing feathers are only on the back edge of the hand and lower arm; the tail feathers are only on the outer rim of the tail.

With all those countable pores, there is good potential for using math skills here. Without actually counting each dot, ask the children to estimate the number of feathers that are on your bird. One standard means of estimation involves opening a paper clip into a square and counting all the pores within that shape. Count the number of times the shape can be placed on the chicken. (Are some areas without pores?) Multiply the number of placements times the number of pores in the first sample. Spend some time brainstorming other possible counting techniques, even if you don't actually do them.

Notice the flap of skin between the sides of the body and the front edge of the wing. Move the wing around to see how it works. Stretched out, the flap becomes a wing edge, then folds out of the way when the bird is at rest. By touching and pinching, notice the stretchability of other areas of the chicken's skin. Compare the skin of the neck and the back, or the hand and the under-arm. Are there differences in flexibility of the skin on our bodies? As you are investigating the skin, look also for the scaly areas at the ankle, just where the foot joins (if you don't have the actual foot to look at). The scaly skin on birds' feet is a fascinating reminder of the ancestral connection to reptiles.

The front edge of the wing formed by the skin flap as it looks on a young crow's wing. The wing has some of the characteristics of a person's arm. The forearm has two bones, and the "hand" is made up of a number of small bones (much simplified in the bird). Notice the lack of muscles in the arm and the way the quills (the covering on the growing feathers) attach directly to the bones.

Fat Deposits and Oil Glands

Fat deposits can usually be seen as yellow globs just under the skin. Fat is stored fuel for the bird to use when food is scarce. For migrating birds and birds that live in cold areas, the fat deposits are essential for survival, providing both insulation and energy. The oil gland, or preen gland, is located at the base of the spine, on top of the tail. As a bird preens its feathers to clean and smooth them, it reaches back to this gland and rubs oil onto its bill. The oil is then applied to the feathers as the bird uses its bill as a preening tool. The preening process of fluffing and arranging the feathers traps air close to the body, insulating and waterproofing the bird. The oil lubricates and strengthens the feathers and is believed to add to the general health of the bird.

Liver (smooth, flabby, dark red organ)

The liver in both birds and humans controls the nutrient content of the circulating blood. It maintains the sugar level, increasing the amount when the bird is stressed by exertion or extremes in temperature. The liver also acts as a filtering system to take wastes from the blood as it circulates through the veins and arteries. The dense, spongy tissue structure is appropriate for the liver's job of mixing and straining the blood.

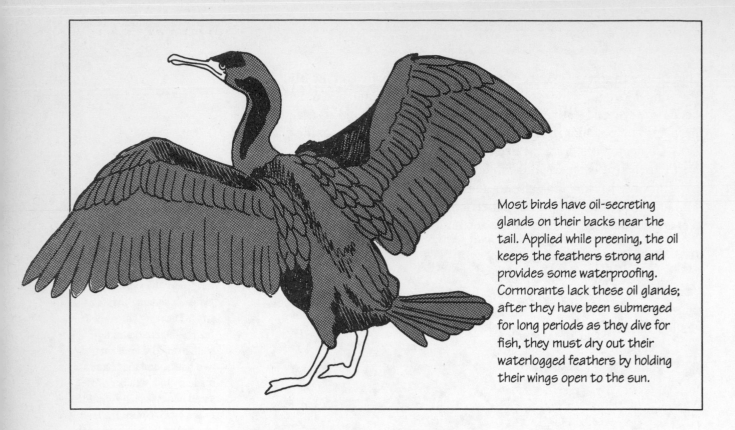

Most birds have oil-secreting glands on their backs near the tail. Applied while preening, the oil keeps the feathers strong and provides some waterproofing. Cormorants lack these oil glands; after they have been submerged for long periods as they dive for fish, they must dry out their waterlogged feathers by holding their wings open to the sun.

Heart (valentine-shaped muscle)

Like a human heart, the bird heart has two sets of paired chambers. One set, on the right, receives the circulating blood, then pumps it out to the lungs for a fresh supply of oxygen. The set on the left receives the renewed blood from the lungs and pumps it out to the body. The heart rate changes according to the bird's activity. A sleeping chickadee's heart pumps 500 times a minute. When the bird is busy at the feeder, its heart is going 1000 times a minute. (How fast are the children's hearts beating as they sit around? After doing thirty seconds of running in place? Each heartbeat is a double thump, the "lub-dub" that can be felt by a hand pressed against the breast bone. The "lub" sound is made when the receiving chambers push the blood into their lower chambers by contracting, like a squeezing fist. The "dub" sound is the contraction of both lower chambers as the right one pushes blood to the lungs and the left one pushes blood to the arteries of the body.)

It might be difficult to slice into the chicken's heart in such a way as to see all four chambers clearly. (A cooked heart tends to be a little easier to slice.) Look carefully at the insides of a chamber, anyway, and note the long fibers of the muscles around it. On top of the heart, you should be able to see several cut veins and arteries, through which the blood enters and leaves the heart.

Gizzard (tough, greyish, lumpy muscle)

Whatever a bird swallows goes down its throat unchewed. (Birds have no teeth. You may have heard of the phrase "scarcer than hens' teeth.") The food sits for a while in a storage area called a crop. The stored food might be regurgitated later to be hidden (jays hide nuts, for instance) or fed to a mate or young. If the food is to be eaten by the bird, it must be ground into smaller pieces; that's the job of the gizzard. The muscular walls of the gizzard are powerful squeezers. With the addition of grit (small stones swallowed by the bird), the squeezing and grinding of the gizzard turns seeds, fruits, insects, or meat into digestible bits. In the stomach, these bits are further reduced by digestive juices until most are absorbed into the circulatory system.

The gizzard you find with a butchered chicken has usually been cut open to clean it, and its irregular shape makes it difficult to reassemble. You may be able to tell the outside wall (shiny with whitish surface) from the inside walls (ribbed and stretchy).

Try to duplicate the grinding action of the gizzard. Put some small, sharp stones (commercial grit for caged birds is sold in grocery stores) and fresh or thawed frozen corn in a heavy-duty plastic bag. What happens to the corn as the bag is pinched and rubbed? Compare the process by repeating the experiment without using the stones.

Neck

The neck of a fryer has lost much of the flexibility the bird enjoyed in life, but you can hold the neck against the body to recreate some of the proportions of a live chicken. (The broader end attached to the body; the narrow end held the head.) The attributes of the neck are interesting in comparison to human neck structures. Both have vertebrae arranged in "strung-bead" fashion, held together by strands of thin muscles. Soft, white nerve tissue, carrying essential information between the brain and the body, can be seen protected within the bones. Large blood vessels pass along just under the muscles, transporting nourishing blood to the brain and the sense organs. (Show the children where to find the pulse in their necks where the blood flows directly up from their hearts.)

TO THINK ABOUT

Discuss the chicken's sense organs, referring to each other's heads for comparison. Ask the children to use their observations of birds to figure out ways the chicken might see, hear, think, or smell scents differently from the ways humans do.

Bird Bills as Tools

Unlike humans and small mammals such as raccoons, birds accomplish important "manual" tasks with their bills, not with their arms or fingers. A bird's arms and fingers are used for flying, as substructures, or frames, for the wings. The work of getting food and building a nest is done mostly with the bird's bill. Talk with the children to find out what they already know about how birds use their bills. Use common examples to trigger memories.

For instance, ask where woodpeckers, owls, ducks, or other common birds get their food; then ask how the bills of each particular species help the bird gather and eat the various foods. Talk about several species until you have named a number of bill uses that are analogous to tools; you might mention chisels (woodpeckers), sharp pincers (owls and hawks), strainers (ducks), straws (hummingbirds), chopsticks (sandpipers), or nutcrackers (seed-eating sparrows). If the children are not familiar with birds, it is crucial that they have pictures to look at as you talk about the different bills. Comparing only two pictures of actual birds is better than talking about birds that children may not ever have seen.

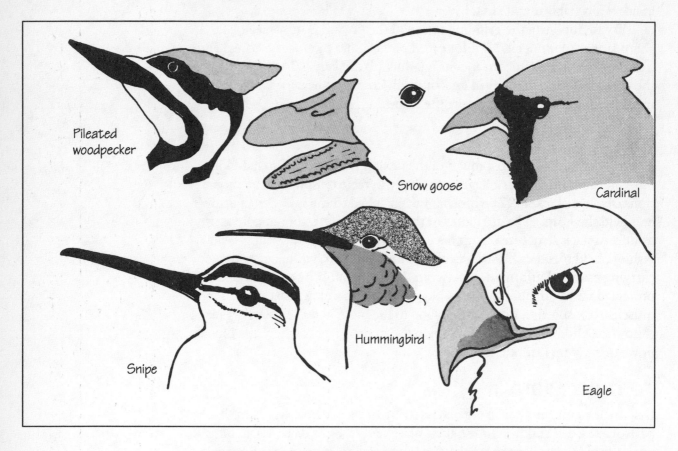

Watch birds feeding outside and talk about the different ways they use their bills. Pigeons, starlings, and house sparrows often feed on the same foods near each other, but their bills are used in different ways. If you can observe the winter feeding of wild birds at a feeder, compare techniques for cracking into seeds. The chickadees hold the seed between their toes and hammer the hull open; the nuthatch jams the seed into a crack and uses its bill to pry and chisel at the hull; most sparrows and finches simply crack the seed by rolling it back and forth over a sharp section of their lower bill, working their bills like pairs of shears or pliers.

After you observe the specific functions of particular bills, show the children birds, or pictures of birds, who have "all-purpose" bills that can be used in several ways. Some of our most common and successful birds have non-specific bill shapes that allow the bird to use a variety of food sources. Crows, jays, and gulls have strong, long, slightly hooked bills. This useful bill, combined with curiosity and intelligence, makes it possible for these birds to live in a variety of habitats.

TO WATCH FOR

Watch birds to see other ways they use their bills. Bills can be used as weapons to drive off other birds. Birds also make clacking sounds with their bills as a warning to others. The behaviors of grooming—cleaning, oiling, and repairing the feathers—are all done by bills. They are also used in courtship rituals (some birds turn their bills to the side when they are making courtship gestures to a prospective mate).

TO DO

- Look around the house or classroom at a variety of tools (hammer, spoon, flyswatter, chisel, straw, chopsticks, pincers, pencil sharpener) and design an imaginary bird that has a bill resembling one of those tools. Each drawing should show the bird in its habitat, using its bill to obtain food.

- Assemble household tools that are analogous to some kind of actual bird bill. (See the list in the previous paragraph.) Gather a variety of foods that birds might eat or that are similar to their foods (cooked spaghetti for worms, macaroni for caterpillars, dried beans for seeds). Think of the attributes of some bird foods and find some household items that are similar (small fish are hard, smooth, and slippery; a small piece of moist soap is similar). Use the tools to "catch" the food. Try to imitate the food-gathering behaviors of actual birds for a full appreciation of their physical and behavioral adaptations.

Darwin's Finches

When Charles Darwin visited the Galápagos Islands, he made a collection of brownish-colored finches, all much alike except for variations in bill shapes and sizes. Each bill clearly had a different use. Darwin could see that there were different species in his finch collection, but he puzzled over their general similarity. Later in his life as a naturalist, he used his collection as an example of the specialization process of evolution. He guessed that a flock of finches had arrived by accident to the islands. There were few other birds there and lots of different sources of food. Although the birds were all the same species, there were naturally occurring differences already present within the original flock, just as there are individual differences in any species.

For the Galápagos finches, slight differences in bill shapes meant that some birds were handier at getting some foods than others. Those young birds that inherited their parents' differences, or that happened to have especially pronounced differences, were better able to exploit an unoccupied feeding niche. Over thousands of years and generations, the new bill shapes and feeding behaviors, along with lack of competition from other birds,

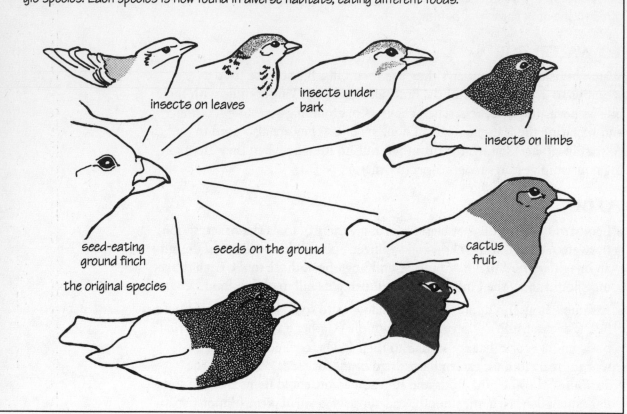

The wide range of finch species found on the Galápagos Islands are thought to have evolved from a single species. Each species is now found in diverse habitats, eating different foods.

insects on leaves

insects under bark

insects on limbs

seed-eating ground finch

seeds on the ground

cactus fruit

the original species

meant greater chances of survival through untapped food sources. The result was seen in Darwin's collection of finches: a variety of bills on similar finch-like birds.

Help the children appreciate the sifting process of natural selection, using examples of birds they know. Woodpeckers, for instance, inherit bill shapes as well as bill behaviors from their parents. (The behaviors are part of the package: A robin born with a woodpecker bill would die.) The young birds that grow strong and find food will live to make more babies the next year. Those that can't get enough food will die. It is a matter of chance—which birds end up with the most efficient bills and behaviors—but it is through those individuals that the species continues. Selection of the best, the fittest, keeps the species going.

But there is another aspect of the evolution game. What would happen if the environment changed, the climate got slowly hotter, the tree and beetle populations changed, and the bills and behaviors that used to work became useless? Every nestful of baby woodpeckers (or new generation of plant or animal) is more or less ready for that eventuality. Because the eggs were made by fertilization, male sperm combining with female ovum, the young will be varied in shapes and behaviors. A variation that may not have worked well on the old environmental conditions (trees and beetles) may work perfectly on the new habitat, and the species can continue.

TO DO

Try out this idea in a playful way. Select a familiar species of bird and ask the children to "evolve" its shapes and behaviors to fit into an environment well known to the children. Try a school playground, a city street, the sewer system, and so on. For instance, a flightless pigeon, a problem in real life, might (with some modifications) survive well as a Ninja Pigeon beneath the streets.

Beaks, Feet, and Bodies:
Adaptations for Survival

Humans have fashioned an amazing variety of tools to extend their natural abilities. From stone hammers to computers, human tools comprise an extraordinary collection. Once children learn that birds' bodies are birds' tools, it becomes a fine game to figure out how particular birds make their living. Help children understand, right from the beginning, that while humans use observation, thought, and planning to make their tools, birds

In the soft mud near a woodland brook or meadow, you will find a set of mysterious clues. By thinking the way a detective thinks, you figure out what the bird might look like, based on the clues.

- Three toes on the foot, like a sandpiper—probably dumpy.
- Tracks close together—short legs.
- Holes in mud go down 3 inches—long bill.
- Then, you draw some conclusions. Since it must probe the mud with its head down, its eyes must be near the top of its head to watch for danger.
- You've never seen such a bird—it must hunt at dusk or dark; it probably has large eyes.
- Plumage probably matches the mottled browns of the earth.

Draw your own version of the mystery bird. Compare with the drawing on page 108.

are born with their tools and the skills to use them. Their body shapes are inherited from their parents, as is their knowlege of how to use their bodies. Try to maintain this distinction between birds and humans as you talk about adaptations. A heron does not have a long beak "so that he can catch fish"; he cannot grow his beak on purpose. Rather, having a long beak enables the bird to catch fish easily. In the same way, a person does not grow tall in order to reach a high shelf (she would, though, be well adapted for playing basketball). People commonly speak as though plants and animals have chosen their physical adaptations in order to accomplish some task or function. Enlist the children in the effort to help each other (and you) stick to the truth. Watch out for the telltale "so that."

Adaptation Games

The following games will increase appreciation for the marvelous and many adaptations we can see among birds. You may wish to present examples of the games initially, to show how each is played, but let the kids take over as soon as possible, doing the research and selecting and devising the new games. They will learn the most by being teachers.

In all the games, the children will divide each bird's adaptations into three units: beak, feet, and body. More complicated divisions may be used with older or more experienced learners.

- **Easy Three-Part Puzzles:** Cut drawings or pictures of familiar birds into three parts (head, body, and feet) and challenge the players to reassemble them. Start a young child out with a single puzzle to assemble, then

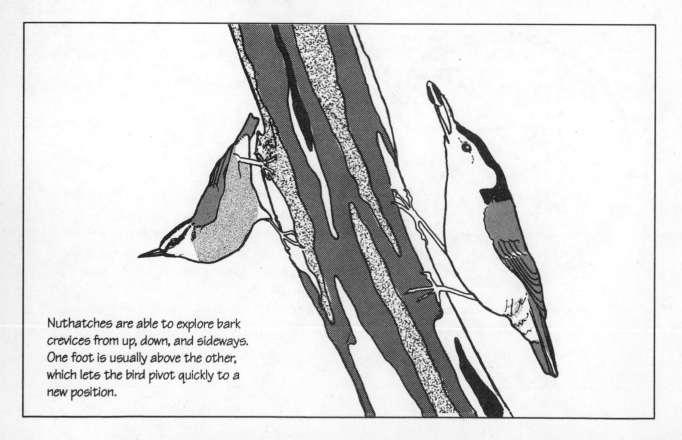

Nuthatches are able to explore bark crevices from up, down, and sideways. One foot is usually above the other, which lets the bird pivot quickly to a new position.

increase the number of puzzles to unscramble as the child gains mastery. As the parts are put together, aspects of each part should be described in relation to the life of the bird. For example, a woodpecker gets its food by searching on trees for insects. Its bill helps it pry under bark and chisel into the wood, its sharp-toed feet enable it to hop up a tree, and the stiff feathers of its tail prop the body as it climbs or hammers.

- **One-page Puzzles:** (1) Match pictures of the beaks and feet of known birds; include descriptions of how each part helps the bird do its work. (2) Create new birds using parts with known uses, for example, create a bird that can make holes in swamp trees while standing in two feet of water, camouflaged as an old tree stump. (3) Draw (or paste on) a picture of a bird with the bill, body, or feet missing. Describe the function of the part to be drawn. (4) Have the children make up their own one-page puzzles.

- **Commercial Ventures:** Make up commercials advertising specific birds as useful household objects. Describe the adaptation of each bird in terms of its superior use for chores around a home. (It's okay to use "so that" with this activity.) For example, doesn't every household need a peacock as a feather-duster? Every time it raised its tail, the walls would be swept of dirt and dust.

- **Mix and Match Book:** Draw or place an illustration of a real or imaginary bird on each page of a book (spiral-bound index cards or writing tablets give the best support and are easiest to handle). Cut each page of the book horizontally into three equal sections. Care must be taken to draw or paste pictures of each bird so that the body parts are aligned on all pages; each

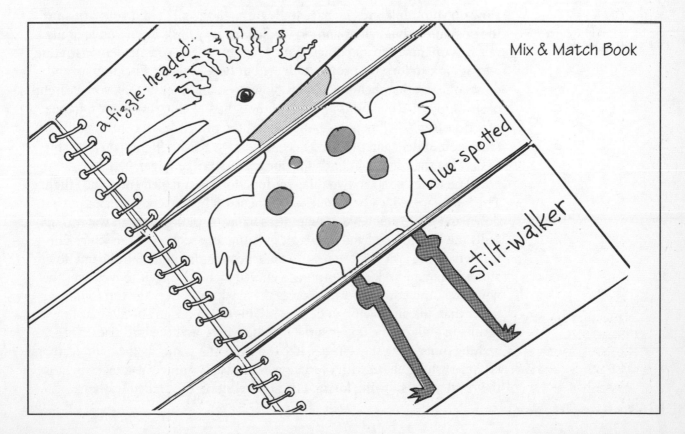

Mix & Match Book

a fizzle-headed

blue-spotted

stilt-walker

bird illustration must be cut at the same junction. By turning the pages a single section at a time, the head, body, and feet of the original illustrations are mixed up, creating new birds with new adaptations. This is a good group project; each person draws one bird within marked guidelines and makes up a name that includes each part. For example, a "pin-beaked, bald-breasted mud wader" on the opening page might become, when the top section is turned, a "trunk-faced, bald-breasted mud wader," and so on.

- **Card Games:** Make up multiple sets of cards, using three cards to represent a known bird (bill and head; feet and legs; body, wings, and tail). The cards are shuffled and dealt, and players try to make complete birds, using the procedures for standard games such as rummy or go-fish. For example, a variety of the game "concentration" can be played by turning the cards face down and having the players turn over three cards at a time, picking up only those cards that make complete birds.

- **Word Birds:** Describe a familiar bird using only one word or phrase to represent each of the three divisions of beak, feet, and body. The guesser must figure out which bird is being described. For instance, a downy (or a hairy) woodpecker might be described by the three terms: chisel, checkers, and climbing spikes. A mallard duck would be described by: strainer, floater, and paddles.

Wings: The Way to Fly

How do you think birds manage to fly through the air? Hold your arms in the position of bird wings and slowly flap the way birds do. If you are only raising your arms up and down from your shoulders, you are demonstrating why it took so long for people to figure out how birds fly. Flapping up and down only works when the wind is blowing straight up. It took some careful observation of actual birds and lots of thought and experimentation (some of it disastrous) before people understood the principles of controlled flight. Once you understand the steps necessary for succesful flight, you'll be able to observe the process in birds that are robin-sized or larger.

The wings perform two different functions in unaided (no wind) flight. The long, tapered feathers attached to the hand bones scoop air and push it down and back, much like a swimmer's hands stroking through water. This pulls the bird forward and draws air over the arm section of the wing. The feathers of the arm section, next to the smooth sides of the bird, bend down at the front and back end, forming a curved arch. As the air moves over the wing arch, the bow of the arch forces the air flowing over the top to move faster than the air flowing underneath. This difference in speed of air flow results in a lift on the upper surface of the wings, and the bird rises. The arching inner wing stays steady, like the wing of a plane, as the hand feathers rotate, pushing ahead with every down-and-back stroke. Sustained flight is the result of this rowing forward to achieve lift on the arched feathers.

The "thumb" feathers, or **alula**, help a bird steer. When raised, they cut the flow of air over the top of the wing, letting a swooping bird slow down enough to land safely. Jet planes use similar devices during landing.

Black-billed magpie

TO DO

Try the following activities to get a feel for flight:

- Use a strip of paper, folded and taped to form a teardrop-shaped wing cross section, to demonstrate the phenomenon of lift. An index card will work; a finger-wide strip of typing paper cut lengthwise is a little more dramatic. Curve the strip into a C-shape, line up the ends, and tape just at the base to hold the ends together. Pinch the lower part of the curve of the paper (see illustration) to make the wing shape: longer arch on the upper side with the shorter, straighter line on the lower side. With a pen or pencil supporting the paper loop, blow across the arch. The "wing" should rise relative to the strength of the air current you create. Turn the shape upside down to test the effect of blowing across the flatter surface.

- Now that you have a sense of the way that the flow of air pulls upward on the arched shape of the arm feathers, try moving your arms as a bird would. Most people hold their arms straight out to imitate wings. This stance gives a look of the appropriate feather length, but does not allow you to move correctly. Starting from the outstretched position, bend your arm and tuck your elbow sharply (and uncomfortably) straight back. It will be more comfortable to bend over with your shoulders in line with your knees; this pose is closer to the position a bird would be in while in flight. On a bird, the upper arm is short and muscular and is held close to the body. The forearm supports the arching feathers and is held away from the body. The hand bones (fewer on birds than humans) control the feathers that scoop

69

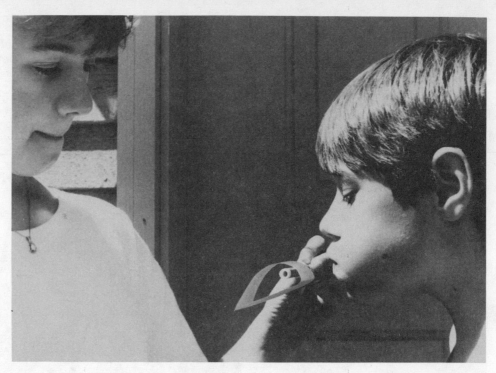

When air is blown over the top of a paper strip shaped like a wing cross section, pressure is reduced on the upper surface and the "wing" lifts.

and push through the air. They can fan out as well as rotate. To be effective scoopers, the hand feathers close together on the down-and-back stroke. As they rotate up and forward, the feathers fan apart, letting the air slip through.

Thumb (alula)

Primaries on "hand"   Secondaries on forearm

■ To fly in the manner of a medium-sized bird such as a robin, the arm moves mostly from the elbow. Hold the elbow steady, away from your body. Start with your forearm and fingers held upward and forward. Close your finger feathers and stroke down and back with a scooping motion. Complete the circular motion with fingers fanned apart until the fingers are up and forward again. It may take you a while to get the hang of it, but it will start to feel right if you think of the fingers as rotating while the arm goes up and down. You will also gain a good idea of which muscles contribute to the flying power of birds.

■ The largest birds tend to flap the least, so if you want to do eagle flight, stretch out your arms and soar through the great rising sweeps of mountain winds. Hummingbird maneuvers in, out, up, down, and around the nectar goblets of flowers require lots of rapid hand movements. It's easiest to do hummerflutters with your hands pulled closer to your body, fluttering them rapidly from the wrist, and "flying" in an upright position, as hummingbirds do. Refer to the illustration of the goshawk and the grouse and act out the way each bird would fly. Add details to the story: the hawk soaring slowly, spotting the crouching grouse that explodes into a rapid but short flight as the goshawk sails toward it through the trees.

Trying out these movements may feel silly, but by trying to fly as birds do, you will be able to observe flight more accurately. You will even understand what Emily Dickinson meant when she wrote that the robin "rowed home."

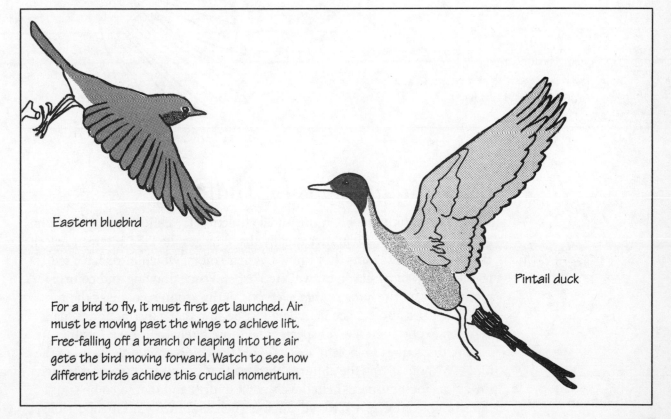

Eastern bluebird

Pintail duck

For a bird to fly, it must first get launched. Air must be moving past the wings to achieve lift. Free-falling off a branch or leaping into the air gets the bird moving forward. Watch to see how different birds achieve this crucial momentum.

TO WATCH FOR

Many birds can be identified on the basis of their flight characteristics (for example, the goldfinch's roller-coaster flight). As you watch the birds in a field, make up your own descriptions of their flight patterns to help you identify birds.

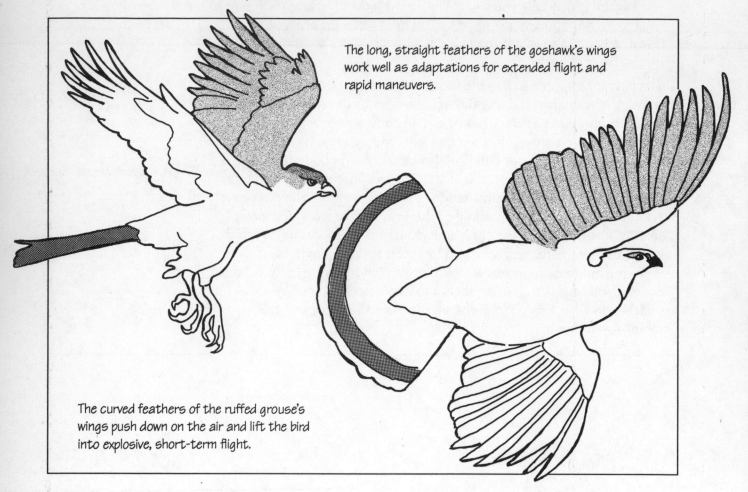

The long, straight feathers of the goshawk's wings work well as adaptations for extended flight and rapid maneuvers.

The curved feathers of the ruffed grouse's wings push down on the air and lift the bird into explosive, short-term flight.

Color Adaptations for Hiding

The colors of birds are often the initial attraction for children. Bright colors give birds a toylike, decorative quality that engages the kids' interest. Ask the children to list the birds they know by their colors: which birds have red feathers (or yellow, black, brown, etc.)? Spend time drawing and coloring pictures of favorite birds so that everyone in the group recognizes them. Exotic species also may be included; just be sure that a distinction is made between exotic (non-native) species and those likely to be seen locally.

With pictures to look at, discuss how the colors might be useful to the birds. Without giving the children the idea that the birds choose or create the colors for a purpose, help the children understand that in some situations bright colors give birds advantages such as showing off to a possible mate, startling a competitor, or signaling to other birds of its kind. You might tell the children that the colorful beaks and throats of begging nestlings stimulate parents to poke food down them, or that when the red spots on the beaks of adult herring gulls are pecked by their young, the adults disgorge food for the babies to eat.

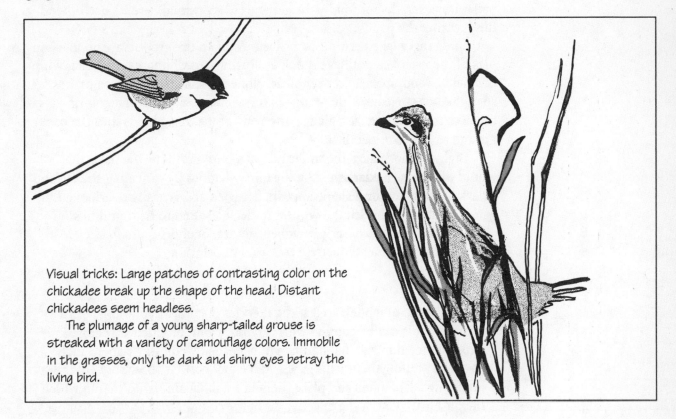

Visual tricks: Large patches of contrasting color on the chickadee break up the shape of the head. Distant chickadees seem headless.

The plumage of a young sharp-tailed grouse is streaked with a variety of camouflage colors. Immobile in the grasses, only the dark and shiny eyes betray the living bird.

Use identification books on local birds to list birds according to colors. As the children notice birds with mixtures of colors, take time to discuss how they might be listed and what advantages the birds might gain from having different colors. The following questions can serve as springboards for discussion of various color patterns:

■ Are colors used in contrasting patterns for their effect? (black cap/white cheeks/black throat on chickadees; black and white patterns on downy and hairy woodpeckers)

■ Are the colors placed where they can be "flashed" when the bird wants to show them off? (the shoulder patches of red-winged blackbirds; colored sections on the wings of some ducks; the gleaming throats and foreheads of hummingbirds)

■ Are the colors hidden until the bird flies? (white wing patches, or "banner patches," on spotted sandpipers, common nighthawks, northern mockingbirds, and shrikes; white outer tail feathers on juncos and towhees)

■ Are the colors accentuated by direct sunlight? (blue colors on blue jays and bluebirds)

The use of color for camouflage is important to your discussion of bird plumage. In some species the females are browner or duller than the males. Harder to see, the female is better protected in her role as the major caretaker of the eggs and young. The colorful male scarlet tanagers and male mallard ducks do not approach the nest at all. (Some differently colored pairs, however, do not follow the general rule: cardinal parents both spend time rearing the young.)

Birds that make their nests or live mostly on the ground are good examples of the use of camouflage. Look at illustrations of pheasants, quail, whippoorwills, sandpipers, and ovenbirds. None are solid brown in color, but are splotched or streaked with a range of brown hues. The uneven coloring tends to trick the eye: at a glance, the body of the bird blends into the background of leaves or pebbles.

Lighter coloring on the underside of a bird brightens the parts that would otherwise be darkened by the bird's shadow. By canceling the effect of a dark shadow, a round shape appears flattened and is easily overlooked. In general, those birds with the whitest undersides tend to be found in sunny, open country such as deserts, beaches, tundra, or short-grass fields. Most plovers and sandpipers illustrate this kind of coloring.

 TO DO

- Make a series of models to test the theories of color adaptations. Cardboard cutouts can be colored with crayons, paint, or glued-on colored paper. Three-dimensional figures can be made by coloring paper lunch bags and stuffing them with paper. Make models that show some of the following adaptations and place them in a habitat similar to that in which the bird lives. Check the effectivness of the coloration at various distances.

- Make models of species that show differences in male and female coloration (tanagers, towhees, cardinals, orioles, ducks, many warblers). See section on plumage differences in male/female birds for more ideas.

- Use paints or markers and a variety of art materials such as sponges and brushes to recreate the effects of mottled camouflage on female ducks, pheasants, sparrows, woodcock, etc. Compare mottled model with a model that is painted solid brown.

- Look at bird illustrations for examples of streaks or patches of contrasting colors that alter the apparent shape of the bird (dark marks on chickadees, killdeer, yellowthroats, etc.). Make up some patterns of your own and try them out on your cardboard models. Compare with an authentic model.

- Using a rounded object for a model, try out the effect of light undersides and dark upper areas. Compare the effect with a second model colored entirely with the same color as the upper area of the first model.

TO WATCH FOR

Pay attention to the occasions when a bird seems to clearly stand out from its surroundings. Might there be reasons for wanting to attract attention? (Perhaps it is defending territory, attracting a mate, or distracting a predator from its young.)

Plumage Differences in Male and Female Birds

Many male birds are easy to find. They sing loudly from prominent perches, move about in eye-catching ways, and sometimes display brightly colored feathers. In contrast, the females of the same species may be more obscure; they often keep closer to cover and are more dull in coloring. In breeding pairs, the behaviors of both males and females contribute to the survival of the offspring.

To understand how different parent behaviors might benefit the young, consider first the sources of danger to the eggs or nestlings. Crows, jays,

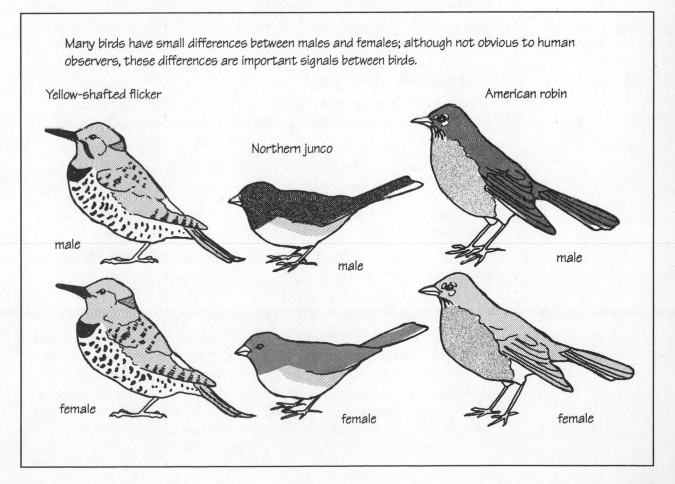

Many birds have small differences between males and females; although not obvious to human observers, these differences are important signals between birds.

Yellow-shafted flicker

Northern junco

American robin

male

male

male

female

female

female

snakes, and cats find prey by sight; female cowbirds recognize nesting activity and lay their eggs in the nests of other birds; birds of the same species sometimes take over the territory of another bird pair. Ask the children how brightly colored, aggressive birds might keep these enemies away? (Consider tactics that threaten *or* divert attention.) How might a quietly colored, quietly behaved parent help its young survive? (Female northern orioles quietly build their nests, while the brightly colored males protect their territory by singing the boundaries and challenging predators.)

The differences in male and female plumage help individual birds find appropriate mates. When a male recognizes a female, he courts her with a series of gestures and vocalizations. The gestures often show off his most colorful feather arrangements. This display not only identifies the bird as male, but also communicates the health and strength of the individual bird. The female will be staking a considerable investment of energy and time in the business of raising a family, and her choice of a partner will be crucial. With little time for choosing and no resumé to guide her, the female judges the male's plumage and performance to determine his potential as protector and provider. One interesting theory points out that outlandish, even predator-attracting displays may be selected as they indicate a greater hardiness in the male bird. Daredevil behaviors (and the tendency to be attracted to such behaviors) may be hereditary in some species, to the extent that some species have adapted to include those tendencies in all its members. Male peacocks, for instance, display cumbersome tails; male mockingbirds sing brazenly.

Species with a Difference

The male and female members of the species in the following list have plumage differences. Use a field guide to help you identify the birds and their markings.

Large differences: mallard duck, cardinal, house sparrow, northern oriole, goldfinch, juncos, rose-breasted grosbeak, red-winged blackbird

Small differences: American robin, mourning dove, hawks, grackles, sparrows, meadowlarks

Hard to detect differences: jays, crows, gulls, Canada goose, chickadees, nuthatches

 **TO DO**

■ The eye-catching effects of brighter colors can be easily tested by hanging paper disks of various colors in a tree or shrub and testing their visibility at increasing distances. Thread, tape, or paper clips can be used to fasten the paper shapes; a strand of thread or string will allow the disk to move in a breeze, creating a livelier model. If possible, match the colors being tested to the colors of species that show plumage differences between male, female, and, possibly, immature birds.

■ Use a bird identification guide to compile a list of those birds and bird groups in which sexual differences in plumage are apparent. Find out about their courtship activities and their roles in raising the young. Are there any correlations? If a pattern is found in several species, can it be used to predict the behavior of another species? Does habitat play a role in predicting bright coloring in the males? (Many tropical birds and birds that migrate to and from tropical areas are brightly colored.)

TO THINK ABOUT

Most bird identification guides position the female birds behind the brighter male birds on the colored plates. This is a common convention, and perhaps it simply represents the common experience of sighting males more easily than females. Ask the children (and yourself) if they have any feeling about the "value" of the female bird implied in the positioning. Would your perception change if the female was in front, for instance? If you were looking for a rare bird species in the outdoors, how would you feel if only the female were sighted? Give the children chances to discuss their feelings without judgment. Look through Audubon's *Birds of America* for non-sexist illustrations.

The female hawk and owl are larger than the male. Perhaps her greater size makes her a good defender of the eggs and nestlings. The difference in size also means that the parents select different sizes of prey from the same environment and, therefore, don't compete for the same prey.

Fast Lives: Metabolism in Birds

Birds are high-speed creatures in every way. They move quickly, they breathe fast, and they gulp their food and digest it within a short period. Even their hearts beat rapidly. Babies grow as large as their parents in about a month and their lives are short, by human standards; the average life span of a bird is about five years. What does growing fast and living fast help a bird do? Help the kids to make a list of answers. Some of the ideas might be: escape predators, capture prey, migrate from the tropics to a good nesting area and raise young and return to the tropics all in one season, escape from stronger rivals in the same species, obtain more of a limited food supply, or search large areas for food or territory.

TO THINK ABOUT

"Fast" is a relative concept. Are there other animals that can do the listed activities faster than birds? How long would it take humans to accomplish the same activities? Are humans generally slower or quicker than birds?

TO DO

The fast-paced life-style of birds is especially interesting in comparison to human attributes. When possible, compare the following statistics on bird physiology with the children's bodies and abilities.

- Have the children count their heartbeats for fifteen seconds. There should be about twenty beats every fifteen seconds. A canary's heart beats 250 times every fifteen seconds, more than ten beats for every one of ours.

- Our normal internal temperature is around 98.6° F. Using a thermometer, have the children mix hot and cold water to create a temperature of 98.6° F in one container and 106° F (the body temperature of a robin) in another container. Test the differences in temperature by placing drops of water on the skin inside the children's wrists or by taking sips. The water that is 98.6° should feel "no temperature" since its heat equals that of the body, while the robin water should feel "hot." Use either "bird" or "people" water to test for temperature sensitivity on other parts of the body. Are any parts of the children's bodies as hot as a bird? How might a person raise his or her body temperature? (Try the water test after one minute of jogging in place.)

- Birds can swallow their food in large chunks. They can get the food into their bodies and then take off to a safe place to digest it. Stored whole in the crop, the food passes to the gizzard where muscular walls and swallowed stones grind the food to a pulp for rapid and thorough digestion. Humans also need to do some grinding before they swallow. An important part of the human digestive process is the predigestive process of chewing. Try chewing thoroughly any starchy food; crackers work well. After even thirty seconds of chewing, notice the increased sweet taste as the starch is changed by saliva into sugar, the basic fuel for all body processes.

■ Sugar energy can be used by the body only as long as oxygen is also present in the blood. To keep the body warm and to fuel the high sugar requirements of flight, birds need lots of air—fast. Birds not only have a rapid breathing rate and large lungs (relative to their small bodies), but they have extra air sacs within their bodies, even within the larger bones. Air that is breathed into the lungs also passes into the air sacs. As the air is breathed out, wastes from the sugar-burning process are expelled. Any unused oxygen coming out of the air sacs is picked up by the lungs as the air passes out of the body. Birds "breathe twice on each breath" since oxygen is available on both inhalation and exhalation. To get some sense of how this all works, measure the children's heart and breathing rates before and after some intensive exercise. Flapping their arms as fast as a crow does in flight should raise their rates sufficiently. Crows flap their wings about two times per second. Do some good, full-winged crow flaps for thirty seconds and record changes and body feelings. Ask the children

In birds, the digestion of food is rapid and thorough. The food is swallowed whole and passes to the gullet. It may be stored there if the food is to be hidden elsewhere or fed to nestlings. Some birds have crops where the food may be stored and softened somewhat. The breakdown of the food begins with the action of the digestive juices in the first stomach, then proceeds with the kneading and grinding action of the gizzard (often enhanced by swallowed sand or grit). The soupy material then passes through the intestines, where the usable fluids are absorbed into the blood; wastes are briefly stored in the cloaca, then ejected through the vent.

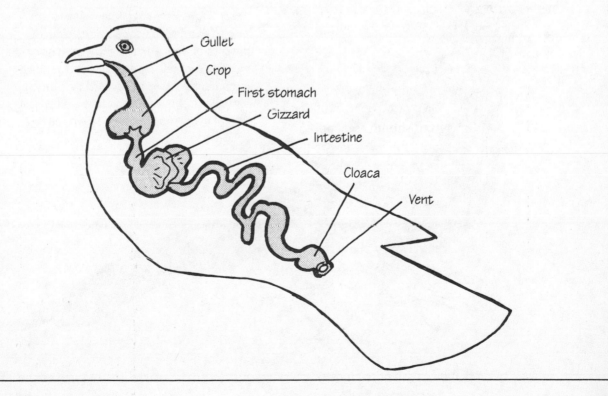

why they think their heart beats faster after exercise. (The muscles in their hearts and chest need more blood. The blood carries sugar, which is food for the muscles, and oxygen.) Are they breathing faster, too?

■ Energy use in animals is something like money use: spending depends on earning (eating). By cutting down on energy spending, birds make the best use of their food. Energy conservation in birds varies with the species and with the season. Discuss with the children ways that they save their energy (resting, sleeping, traveling on bicycles, wearing warm clothes in winter and cool clothes in summer) and search for analogies with bird life. The children might enjoy drawing cartoons showing comparable energy-saving ploys by kids and specific birds. Some of the analogies might be:

-*Coasting down hill*—Many large predator birds (hawks, eagles, gulls, and others that search from the air) catch rides on rising air and soar without flapping their wings. The birds with the longest wings are the best coasters.

-*Resting at night and at midday*—Birds seem to need little sleep; while migrating or when nesting in the nightless summer of the Arctic, they sleep very little. In general, birds rest during dark hours and slow down during midday. Short rests during the day save a bird some energy and effectively hide it from the eyes of a predator.

-*Keeping warm with thick coats or cover*—All birds have automatic down parkas. When the overlapping body feathers are fluffed up, the down

Desert nights are cold. Roadrunners are able to warm themselves by exposing patches of dark skin and feathers to the morning sunlight. By absorbing solar energy, a roadrunner reduces its need to burn fats for fuel. Patches of featherless skin on the belly of many birds let eggs be warmed by body heat.

feathers and air underneath become a layer of insulation, trapping body heat. Winter birds also seek cover in storms or during the night, often huddling together to minimize exposure to the cold. Several species are know to fall into a deep sleep during cold nights. Briefly hibernating, their body temperatures are so low that little energy is used.

-Eating high-calorie foods—Most birds cannot survive on a diet of leaves, as many mammals and insects do. Birds need high-octane fuels such as seeds or meats (mammals, other birds, reptiles, amphibians, insects, or fish).

TO WATCH FOR

Find out if birds really are more active in the morning than during midday. Spend fifteen minutes birdwatching morning and again at noon, listing all the species you hear and see. When did you see more birds and what were they doing?

Variation within a Species

Most bird identification books show pictures of just one coloration pattern for each species, including both male and female if they are differently colored. If you could see a collection of birds of the same species, however, it would be obvious that all birds of the same species are not exactly alike.

Variation of form within a species is a rule of nature. When a bird such as the rufous-sided towhee has a country-wide range, differences can be seen among local populations. Western birds have more white spots than eastern towhees, and southern birds can have white or red eye colors.

Some differences are relative to age or sex. Birds that live in different areas may also look different. Even among birds that hatch from the same nest, slight differences occur. In nature, variations on a pattern are the rule.

Ask the children to think of animals they have seen that look different but still are members of the same species. Domestic animals show these variations more clearly than wild animals. For thousands of years people have been creating varieties through selective breeding that enhances natural differences. The many shapes and colors of dogs, cats, sheep, cows, and horses are the result of human selections. Any flock of city pigeons shows natural variations. If you can find pictures of fancy domestic pigeons, you can see how those characteristics have been exaggerated by selective breeding.

Even birds that look exactly alike at a human glance can be distinguished as different by birds themselves. In any flock of gulls, starlings, sparrows, crows, or chickadees, individual differences among the birds determine a hierarchy or pecking order. By marking the individuals, people have been able to see that each bird has a place in its social group. Certain birds will be chased away by some members of the group, but those birds may safely chase *other* birds in the group. Being able to recognize each other and learn social standing means that injuries are limited. Less bloodshed occurs because each bird knows its place relative to the others and does not waste energy to prove its strength repeatedly. Bird pairs may have the same or a different place in the hierarchy. Females in flocks, such as hens, have their own strict pecking orders. In crow societies, a female takes the social position of her mate.

In terms of food, mating, and territory, variation in a species means that the stronger individuals will be winners. If the resources are limited, these individuals are the most likely to defend territories and produce offspring, and the strong traits of that species will be passed on. Natural variation has significance in regard to outside influences as well. If the environment were to change in some significant way, individuals that may not previously have been "the best" may have some characteristic that works well in the new environment. The environment, in effect, limits the survival of some characteristics and enhances the survival of others. Without variation within a species, any change in environment could destroy the species altogether.

This phenomenon is easiest to find among insects that reproduce rapidly and abundantly. For example, a species of tree-resting moth that previously showed a nearly even mixture of mostly grey or mostly white adults changed over a few years to mostly dark individuals. A study of their environment revealed that industrial pollution was darkening the trunks of trees. The white moths were clearly visible against the bark and were eaten by birds before they could reproduce. The dark moths were overlooked by the birds and survived to reproduce. After laws for pollution control were put into effect, the trees grew cleaner and the white moth variation returned (the grey moths still carried genes for the white color).

All our house sparrows are the offspring of parent flocks brought to the United States from Europe. (It was hoped that they would eat up caterpillar pests; instead, they are pests themselves, aggressively driving off native birds that would have done the job better.) They now live in a wide variety of habitats throughout the continent. Each new generation of sparrows faced the predators, food limitations, and weather conditions of the different habitats. Some birds had variations that allowed them to deal with the conditions better than others. For instance, lighter-colored birds keep cooler in desert areas; birds with larger bodies are better at saving body heat in northern regions. Even after only a hundred years, entire populations of house sparrows from different parts of the country show some of these adaptations. (They also show variations that we can't explain. Populations vary whenever they are isolated from each other.)

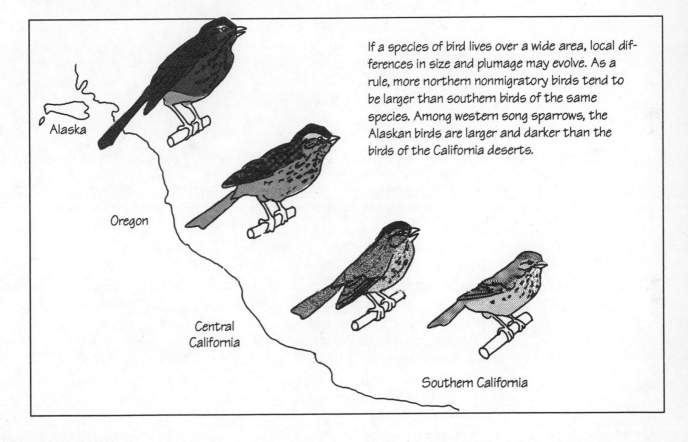

If a species of bird lives over a wide area, local differences in size and plumage may evolve. As a rule, more northern nonmigratory birds tend to be larger than southern birds of the same species. Among western song sparrows, the Alaskan birds are larger and darker than the birds of the California deserts.

Alaska

Oregon

Central
California

Southern California

TO DO

The following activities are designed to call attention to the widespread evidence of species variation in nature. Any naturally occurring population of trees or flowering plants will show differences within the species. Pick and compare same-species samples of common plant materials: oak, maple, or willow leaves; daisy, dandelion, or clover blossoms; seeds or fruit. Note variations in color, shape, or texture.

- A traditional standby activity about individual differences (and our ability to perceive them) involves having each person choose an apple or an orange from a bowl, spend time getting to know the chosen item (sketching reveals many details), then returning it to the bowl. Blindfold each participant and ask them to choose their own fruit from the bowl. Even blindfolded, most people have little trouble finding their fruit.

- Similar activities can be done outdoors. Pine cones, tree leaves, or any pods or seeds with irregular shapes can be chosen. Be forewarned that once children become "friends" with their items, they will want to keep them.

PART FOUR

BEHAVIOR: BIRDS IN ACTION

Making friends with birds is a large part of the experience of birdwatching. Once the preliminary introduction is made ("Birdwatcher, this is Mrs. Mallard"), the subsequent information you gather forms a series of connecting links. You will discover where the bird lives, how it acts at different times of the year, and what it does for a living. These and other facts will add to your awareness of the lives of birds, whether they are common neighbors or exotic celebrities.

Birds always seem to be up to something. Every day birds must get enough to eat and drink, watch out for danger, keep their feathers in good condition, and find a safe place to sleep. Depending on the demands of the season, they may be migrating, maintaining territories, attracting or selecting a mate, nest-building, caring for young, or dealing with life in a flock.

Once a watcher learns to identify the basics of bird behavior, every bird has a story to tell. The story may be a variation on a typical life history or a chance, unique event in the life of that particular bird. It's easy to start. You will learn a great deal just by asking simple, open-eyed, open-minded questions—like "What on *earth* is that bird *doing*?"

Watching
Bird Behavior

Identification through Behavior

If you only look at the pictures in a field guide, you might think that identifying birds depends on learning the shapes and patterns of feather colors. The use of markings to distinguish species can be difficult for a person new to birdwatching; each new bird must be "caught" by the binoculars while its streaks, stripes, bars, and eye rings are compared to the illustrations in the field guide

Although an initial study of markings is important, you will eventually become familiar with many species, and you may even identify some of them by characteristic gestures, just as a friend is known by a special walk or way of eating. The text of your bird book may be especially helpful at this stage. Gestures that distinguish the bird (flight rhythms and feeding or hunting behaviors) are discussed in most bird books. The most helpful habit for learning bird behavior is to report what you see. The report can be notes in the margin of your bird guide, a letter to an interested friend, a "news" article, a birdwatching diary, or a simple form similar to the example on the following pages. The discipline of capturing the observations in words actually makes the observer more aware of the behaviors of the birds. Writing down what you see also makes the memory more accessible to you at a later date.

Birds can be hard to see except during activities that require them to move. They must get food, defend a territory, attract a mate, and respond to perceived danger. Flying is usually related to one of those needs (migration is a combination of the first and second needs).

Learning to recognize birds is similar to learning to recognize music, except the "tunes" in birdwatching are visual rhythms and thematic patterns of action and reaction. While you observe birds, keep the questions that follow in the back of your mind. Obtaining the answers will help you develop your sense of familiarity with each species you see.

Feeding Behaviors

- How does the bird feed?

- Does it search close to its food source or does it watch from afar?

- Is it walking, hopping, or trying to flush prey by movement?

- Does it fly to the prey or stalk it?

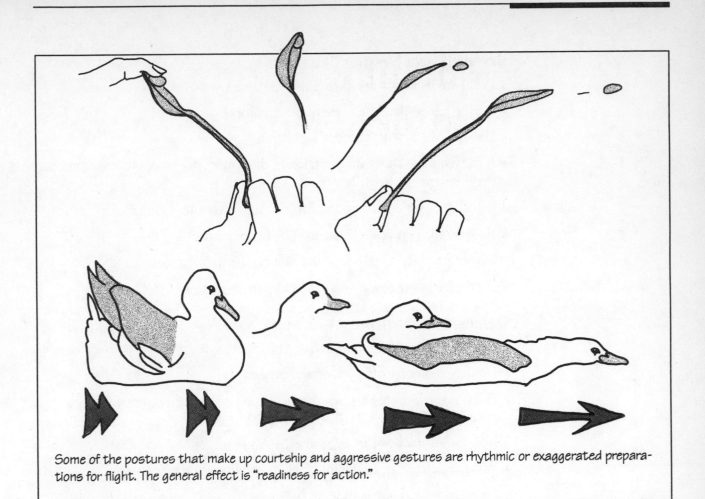

Some of the postures that make up courtship and aggressive gestures are rhythmic or exaggerated preparations for flight. The general effect is "readiness for action."

- Can it move in a leisurely manner because its food is a plant or an animal too small to be aware of it?
- Does it use its bill as a tool?
- Does it use its talons?
- Does it feed by itself or in a flock?
- Do these habits change with the seasons?

Interactions with Other Birds

- What are its interactions with other birds of its species?
- Does it move in a flock?
- How does it assert itself?
- Does it make special flocking sounds?
- Does it display striking color patterns at particular times?
- Do its courtship gestures remind you of anything you have seen elsewhere?
- How does it signal appeasement?

Breeding and Nesting Behaviors

- What are its behaviors during the breeding season?

- Do the sexes share the same responsibilities?

- How are the nesting materials gathered?

- If the female is the main caretaker of the young, does her plumage express the difference in her role?

- What behaviors of the parent birds change after the young hatch?

- How do the young stimulate feeding in the adults?

- Do young birds remain near the nesting site to form a winter flock?

- Do the breeding adults migrate before their young?

Defensive Behaviors

- How do the birds respond to danger?

- Do they mob or scold a suspected predator?

- What is the form of their aggressive displays: sharp cries, crest feathers raised, tail flicking, bill snapping, diving?

- In what season was the defensive display observed?

- Was the defense of young birds the motivation for the response?

Maintenance Behaviors

- What are the patterns of feather maintenance?

- What gestures accompany water bathing: preening, scratching with the foot?

- Is dust used for bathing?

- Are ants involved in an apparent dust bath?

- When is evidence of molting observed?

Taking Bird Notes

The format of the sample note page that follows will help you begin to record your observations of bird behavior. Many of the behaviors can be filled in after only one observation session. You might look up the answers *before* going out so you know what to look for. Don and Lillian Stokes's three guides to bird behaviors will provide answers to most of the questions for the more common species in North America. The first volume, *A Guide to the Behavior of Common Birds,* contains all the species discussed in the "Common Birds to Watch For" section of this book. Feel free to copy the note page and use it to record information on every bird you observe. In field use with children, the note page is very helpful in focusing the interests (and energies) of individual or small groups of kids.

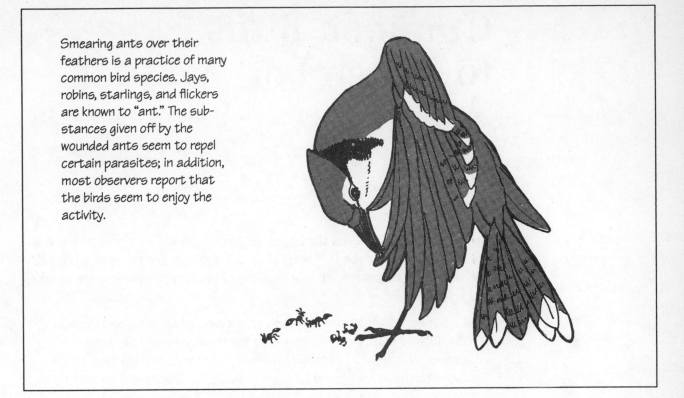

Smearing ants over their feathers is a practice of many common bird species. Jays, robins, starlings, and flickers are known to "ant." The substances given off by the wounded ants seem to repel certain parasites; in addition, most observers report that the birds seem to enjoy the activity.

Bird Observation Notes

NAME OF BIRD_____

DATE _____

OBSERVATION LOCATION _____

IDENTIFICATION HINTS What sounds or behaviors help in finding this bird?

HABITAT Describe the habitat. In which parts of the habitat does the bird spend its time?

FEEDING Describe how the bird acts when it is getting food. Include any interactions with other birds.

FLIGHT How close will the bird let people approach? Does it have a special alarm call? Do any bright patches of feathers (banner patches) show when the bird flies? Is there anything characteristic about its flight?

AGGRESSION What threatening behaviors are observed? Describe the interactions. What does the bird do to announce or defend a territory?

COURTSHIP/MATE-BONDING What interactions look like courtship gestures or pre-nesting activities?

FAMILY LIFE What interactions look like a parent caring for its young or a young bird begging for food?

OTHER ACTIVITIES (MIGRATION, FLOCKING, ROOSTING) Describe any other behaviors you observe.

Common Birds to Watch For

Blue Jays

The jays of North America tend to be very noticeable. Their group behavior is noisy, and they are the first birds to spot a predator (or birdwatcher) and start scolding. The following observations of blue jays provide some insight into jay behavior:

- On a winter morning, two jays flew into a dense juniper tree. A mocking bird followed close behind them. One jay emerged from the upper branches and flew to a nearby fence post. As the second jay flew to the fence with the mockingbird in close pursuit, the first bird flew past them, drawing the mockingbird back to the juniper. The jays continued to fly back and forth from tree to fence several times, the mockingbird in constant chase. Finally, the jays flew away together, leaving the mockingbird on the fence post, slow-flicking its tail.

Blue jays (and their relatives) have a habit of harvesting tree seeds and transporting them to hiding places within their territories. Forgotten seeds may sprout into trees, creating new forests and food for future generations of jays.

■ The call of a red-tailed hawk from the depths of a maple woodland seemed unusual, but there was no doubt of the sound. A closer look revealed a blue jay, speaking perfect hawk.

■ In late summer, a lone jay was observed to be repeatedly gliding down a narrow, wooded gorge that sloped to a pond. The slope was a favorite of winter sledders because the dense shrubs along the path gave a wonderful sense of speed. Like the sledders, the jay would return to the upper slope slowly, flying from shrub to shrub, then glide down toward the pond, calling loudly.

■ Out walking after a week of unusually frigid days, a walker observed a house sparrow begin a flight over a small field. Suddenly a blue jay over took the sparrow, grabbed it with its feet, and glided heavily into a thicket, out of sight. The sparrow's alarm cries, which had begun when the jay overtook it, stopped abruptly.

■ Following the sound of alarmed chickadees, a walker arrived in time to see the parent birds diving at a jay that was reaching into their nesting cavity. The baby within reach of the jay was a half-grown cowbird. As the walker approached, the jay dropped the baby and flew away.

■ The sound of yelling jays could be heard all through the pine forest along the river. More jays flew in the direction of the screaming mob. In the center of the mob was a great horned owl, flinching and ducking as jays brazenly dived at the large bird.

■ In the summer twilight, a girl discovered a fledgling jay baby settled on a branch near her house. Pulling a lawn chair under the tree, she reached up and gently picked the little bird off the branch. The young jay began to call for help, and within moments every bird in the neighborhood seemed to arrive to scold and yell at her. The baby was released to flutter off, but the adult birds continued to fuss until the girl disappeared.

■ On a spring walk through an overgrown orchard, an observer was struck by the silence of the jay that moved off at her approach. Why would the jay not sound an alarm? In a nearby thick tangle of honeysuckle vines, the dense shape of a jay nest was found.

■ On an August dawn the summer singers were quiet, but suddenly the tree near the house sounded as if it were full of little pumping machines, creaking and squeaking. The sight was even more perplexing: a flock of jays were making the sounds. A jay would pump its body up and down making a "tee-dee-lee" call with each pump. At one point, all the birds stopped their sounds and movement and flew off together. These birds were exhibiting the behaviors of a courting coterie, a group of displaying males led about by a female bird.

Observers with special equipment and particular questions in mind have been able to mark individual jays and find out more nifty details about jays. For instance, bird experts have noted that jays are major movers in transporting large (not airborne) seeds of trees. When nuts such as acorns are ripe, jays will flock to the area and bring large quantities back to their territories, where they hide them under leaves on the ground. Since jays can nest in young-growth pines (one of the first trees to grow in areas of reforestation), jays may well have been responsible for the rapid return of hardwood forests to glaciated areas of North America.

Careful tracking of jays has also revealed that yearling jays sometimes stay around and help with the raising of the next summer's young. Success in nature depends upon the survival of offspring, as well as individual survival. The instinct to help with the care of younger siblings probably increases the size of the "family" and also provides parenting experience for the yearling jays.

Chickadees

Chickadees are hardy little packets and are clever enough to survive cold mountain and northern winters. Usually found scouting around in dense thickets or evergreen forests, they will often approach people, seemingly out of curiosity. If you hang out a new birdfeeder or fill an old feeder for the first time in the fall, a chickadee will probably be the first bird to notice.

At the end of the summer, a breeding pair and their offspring will form

In early spring, the wintering flocks of black-capped chickadees begin to break up into breeding pairs. When you see a bird (the female) wing-flutter like a fledgling as another bird (the male) feeds it, you know spring is on its way.

the basis of a winter flock. The summer residents of your area may migrate a short distance southward, and your wintertime chickadees may be a family flock from farther north. The simple, whistled "dee-dee" of the spring song can be heard on any sunny day after winter solstice. Listen carefully. Some birds sing three notes (the second tone is doubled). Watch for winter chickadees (and titmice) with bent tail feathers—these result from cramming into tree cavities with the rest of the flock for warmth through the winter nights.

Chickadees peck out their own nesting cavities from soft, rotten branches or small tree trunks, often at about two feet from the ground. You might have better luck attracting chickadees to a birdhouse if the house is packed with fresh wood shavings so that the birds can shape the cavity to their liking. If a chickadee is approached while sitting on its nest, it may produce a startlingly snakey hiss.

Grackles

For people in northern North America, the first sign of returning spring weather is the sight of grackles. In the southern states, wintering grackles may be visible year-round, hunting in fields and yards or noisily "grackling" together in the treetops. Grackles live in groups throughout the year. During the nesting season the groups are often small and are characterized by clus-

Shortly after arriving on their breeding grounds, small flocks of the larger male grackles start following the females around. When on the ground, the males display with feathers fluffed and bills raised. While flying, they call and spread their tails. Eventually, only one male follows the female and the pair is formed.

ters of nests near each other in tall evergreens. As soon as breeding duties are done, the small groups gather together in large groups. In the fall, the route from a late-afternoon feeding place to the night roost may be a dense stream of flying birds, as much as twenty wingspans wide, stretching in length from horizon to horizon. An observer might watch this whirring blackbird river flow overhead for a half-hour or more. When the birds are finally gone, the sky seems very quiet.

In courtship as well, grackles are noisy and obvious. Several male grackles may loudly pursue a single female. As they fly, the males fan their long tail feathers into V shapes. If the female lands, the males stride around her, alternately fluffing out and sleeking down their iridescent neck feathers and pointing their beaks upwards. Each fluffing pose is accompanied by a squeaky-sounding "sckleek." Eventually only one male follows a female, and the pair begins to gather grasses for nest-building. Once the eggs are laid, the male may seek out another female and begin another nest and family.

Gulls

In some ways making a living by the edge of the water is much like making a living on the edge of a city. Various species of gulls have become numerous around human habitats, both coastal and inland. Large flocks hunt over landfills and parking lots, using their habits of scavenging along beaches and

Where gulls gather, there is always interesting behavior to watch. The gull on the far right is defending his space by calling long and loud at the gull flying by. The two gulls near each other are sorting out their relationship with bill-pointing and neck-stretching gestures. The bird pointing down is mildly threatening; the upright bird is standing its ground.

riverbanks to find edible trash of all sorts. At one time gull populations were severely threatened by people wanting gull feathers for hats and gull eggs for breakfast. Now gulls are considered overabundant and a threat to the eggs and nestlings of smaller shorebirds. Look for the following gull behaviors and consider how these habits have preadapted the birds to living off thrown-away flotsam:

- **Cruising for food:** A gull's sleek body and long wings are good adaptations for slow, soaring flight while searching for food items. In their natural habitat, food can include washed-up plant material, carrion, eggs, or live mollusks. Gulls learn to go to food that looks like litter.

- **Eating habits:** The main gull utensil is a long, strong bill that can be used for tearing, prying, and probing. Its large size allows the gull to gulp down large items, which is usually a good strategy since it keeps other gulls from stealing the food. Gulls also learn to acquire food that comes in containers (clams, mussels, half-opened tuna cans) by dropping it on a hard surface. Paved roads, parking lots, and flat roofs are often littered with cracked (and empty) shells or containers.

- **Watching each other:** If a soaring gull makes a dive after food, other gulls will quickly converge on the spot. The white feathers and underwings of a soaring adult bird can be seen for miles even on cloudy days.

Mallard Ducks

Most public parks with ponds come complete with several mallard ducks. The coloring on the male is usually bright and distinct: shiny green head, chestnut breast, white flanks, tidy white neck ring, and nifty little curly feathers over the tail. The plumage of the female mallard is mottled brown, and her tail feathers do not curl. When she sits quietly on her nest among dry leaves, she is very hard to see. It is something of a surprise to find that she has the louder voice of the pair. The loud, descending "Qua-qua-qua" is the female, uneasy at being separated from her mate. The male's response is likely to be his quieter, drawn-out "Rheh." Since most white pond ducks are descendants of mallards, their sexes can be distinguished on the same basis of voice and the male's curly tail feathers.

Having sorted out the male and female mallards by their colors and voices, look for some pairing behaviors. Ducks do much of their courtship during the winter months and can be easy to observe in a park pond, but the behaviors are very quick. Many gestures are accompanied by calls. The male may whistle, and the female may rapidly call "queh, queh. . . ." Male courtship displays consist of quick, ritual-like gestures of head shaking, neck stretching (upward or arching down), or head bowing. The actions may seem like preening or bathing actions. The clue is in the context. Groups of males may be displaying to females, or a pair may be responding to another duck swimming toward them. The female responds to intruders with rapid head turns, usually as she swims near her mate.

During the early summer nesting period, the female seems to disappear, but actually she is carefully hidden, occupied with caring for the eggs and then the young. She may join her mate occasionally in their small "resting territory," a portion of shore and water they defend as their mutual domain. The male seems to disappear in late summer, but he has actually undergone a partial molt, and his new colors are similar to the female's. In fall, he will molt again and begin courting in early winter with a new set of bright feathers.

Once the mallard ducks have formed pairs in the fall, they respond as a team to events around them. The female responds to threats (other ducks, predators) with loud quacking and a series of quick, over-the-shoulder head turns. This gesture incites the male to swim toward the threat, often with his neck and bill held low over the water.

Mockingbirds

A mockingbird singing from the top of a tree or house is a childhood memory for many people. So is the frightening tyranny of a backyard mockingbird who tries to drive children and pets out of its summer nesting areas. Both behaviors epitomize the aggressive nature of mockingbirds. The male's spring song, loud and varied, proclaims his willingness to fly at any interloper. The courtship chases of male mockingbirds after females look more like aggression than attraction. The singing and attacking diminish by the end of the summer, but singing resumes in the fall as mockingbirds stake out their winter territories. This time the enemy targets are the jays, robins, and blackbirds that might eat the same winter berries and seeds as the mocker.

In addition to a loud and varied repertoire of songs, the mockingbird accentuates its presence by performing a geyser-flight straight up and then fluttering down, all the while singing.

If you can find a mockingbird to watch, look for some of these behaviors that indicate territorial defense:

■ A mockingbird is most likely to sing toward his territory. You may be able to detect his boundaries by carefully listening to the loudness of his song. If you are "behind" his voice, you are probably on the edge of his territory. Any interloper who flies into the mockingbird's "song beam" knows he's in trouble.

■ The older the singer, the more varied and complicated the song. Mocking birds incorporate sounds around them into their repertoire. A bird living by the shore might sing plover and gull calls; an inland bird will probably sing variations on woodland bird song. There is no evidence that the birds being mimicked are scared away by the sound.

■ The white panels that show on the spread wing and tail feathers seem to enhance many of the mockingbird's behavioral displays. While singing, a male may fly straight up and flutter down, white banners flashing. The bottom of a dive is often accented by fanned-out wings and tail. Before or after aggressive displays, a mockingbird will stand with drooping wings or slowly whisk its tail up and down: the white glimmers like a slow fire.

■ A mockingbird standoff is an impressive example of powers in balance. In such a display two mockingbirds move haltingly alongside each other. Occasionally one will show a flick of white by drooping its wings, slow-flicking its tail, or even raising its wings in a jerky, circular motion. The action is usually repeated by the other bird. These birds are at the edges of their territories, walking the boundary, keeping the peace mockingbird-style.

Pigeons

The next time you see pigeons in a city setting, try to imagine that the tall buildings behind them are looming sea cliffs, the sidewalk pavement is a rocky beach, and the surge of traffic and people is a coursing river that flows to the sea. With a little imagination, you can understand why municipal centers are ideal habitats for rock doves, the European name for our common pigeons. Edible trash, open parks, and the ledges on buildings are ideal components of a pigeon habitat. Some people breed pigeons, using them for food, for racing, for study of bird navigation, or for competitive breeding of rare variations. Some people keep pigeons just for the pleasure of watching their flock wheel and soar high over the city.

To sharpen your awareness of pigeon behavior, try to observe the following:

Attention-getting strut of the male bird. The bill is pulled down onto the fluffed-up breast feathers, the wings are lowered slightly, and the tail is

Since pigeons breed throughout the year, courtship behavior can occur whenever a flock gathers. The courting male distinguishes himself with fluffed-out breast feathers and dance struts and by fanning and dragging his tail feathers. Although the performance is directed at a particular female, she usually shows little change in her behavior.

fanned and dragged while the bird walks in tight circles in front of another (probably female) bird.

Wing clapping in flight. As a flying bird leaves or nears its fellow flock members, the wing feathers are hit together like clapping hands. Usually done by mature birds, the behavior has a "look at me" quality.

Drinking with heads down. Most birds must tilt their heads back to drink, but pigeons are able to drink with their heads down. Pigeon young drink digested food from their parent's crop, a behavior that is also demonstrated by courting adults.

Red-winged Blackbirds

Red-winged blackbirds are the most numerous of all bird species in North America. Dense flocks of redwings winter in southern coastal marshes and grain fields. In the spring the redwings are among the first to return to the thawing marshlands. Flocks of breeding males arrive first and immediately begin to claim nesting territories. The females come later and have usually chosen their mates by the time the yearling birds arrive.

The territories within the wetland shrubs and cattails are at a premium, and the males do a great deal of vocalizing and displaying of their red shoul-

The coloring and behaviors of male and female red-winged blackbirds make them seem almost separate species. The male is aggressive, easily seen, and easily heard. The female is well camouflaged and secretive.

der feathers in their efforts to claim good patches of land. A good territory can mean more progeny, as several females will breed with one male if he is able to secure a rich territory.

The late summer cattail marsh is much quieter. The redwings may still be there, but they are more secretive during their molting period. By fall the winter season flocks begin to form. The males, females, and immature birds tend to keep separate company. These same-sex and same-age subgroups may make up very large flocks that roost in the same area at night and leave to feed in several areas in the morning. The subflocks hunt and feed in their own special feeding places until sunset. This pattern probably benefits all the birds, especially the inexperienced young. The nights are spent in the comparative safety of large numbers, and the confident morning departure of older birds to a known food source draws other birds along to good feeding grounds.

Robins

Where did robins live before humans came along and created lawns? Robins prefer to hunt for insects in short grass or disturbed soil; neither grassy fields nor deep woodlands will do. They must have been common sights around Native American settlements, readily expanding into the European-style farmlands of the colonists who named them after the wrenlike, red-breasted robin of the Old World.

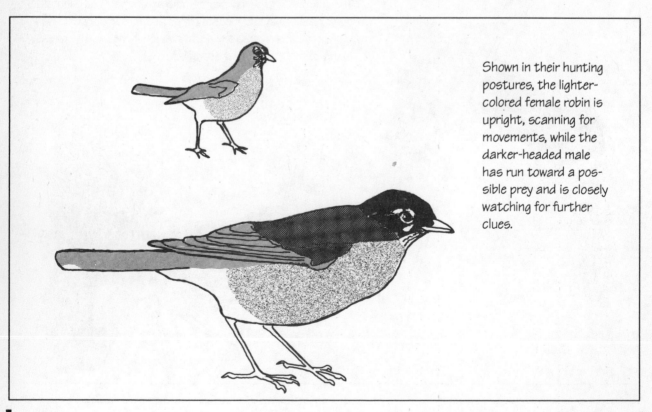

Shown in their hunting postures, the lighter-colored female robin is upright, scanning for movements, while the darker-headed male has run toward a possible prey and is closely watching for further clues.

The American robin is a thrush, and, like other thrushes, it builds mud-lined nests, hatches light blue-green eggs, and has speckled-breasted young. Most suburban dwellers have seen robins. The nests are often built near enough to dwellings to be easily observed, and the summer robin chorus, especially at dawn and dusk, is common throughout North America.

Feeding behavior is conspicuously carried out in the middle of lawns. The movements are similar to those of mockingbirds or shorebirds such as plovers. The hunting bird makes a brief run forward, stops abruptly, and watches for movement of prey. A possible movement is checked out by one eye, with the side of the head cocked toward the object. A shiny shape means earthworm or insect to a robin, and the sparkle alone may trigger a robin to pounce. Cellophane or plastic waste may fool a hunting bird, and robins have been found to suffer from plastic-blocked digestive systems.

Starlings

Watch starlings interact as they sit along a ledge of a building or in a line on a wire. They sit near each other but never closer than about the space of one starling (close enough to reach across with a sharp bill but far enough that a jab can be avoided). The noisy hassling you may observe is typical of many

As the starlings gather into their wintering flocks, their plumage appears spotted with speckles, a scattering of stars, against a black background. As breeding season approaches, the feathers show only a glossy, iridescent blackness.

flocking birds. Though the bickering may seem mean, serious harm seldom occurs. The ongoing aggression and compliance create a flexible hierarchy. When disputes occur over choice nesting sites, mates, or food, the established dominance of some birds makes fighting less necessary. The underlings go elsewhere.

Despite their raucous squabbles, order dominates the life of a starling. Flocks of starlings choose particular places for nighttime roosting. Sometimes many flocks, totaling thousands of birds, will return to the chosen roost every night (except for incubating females). The starlings also have set routes for traveling to roosts or feeding areas, and within these routes are established lanes for going and returning.

Their natural abilities as scavengers, their aggression in taking over nesting sites from other species of birds, and the protection of the flock combine to make starlings successful in many areas of the world. Wherever people live untidily, wherever city or rural wastes are available, starlings are noisily abundant.

General Behaviors: Interacting with the Environment

A Singing Bird

Why do birds sing? Think of examples of when and why people sing. Discuss which of those situations might apply to birds. Our best clues to why birds sing come from observing when birds sing and what other birds do in response to the singing. What have the children already observed?

Birds sing the most in the spring. Migratory birds sing during migration and continue as they arrive in their breeding area; species that winter in their breeding area may have been singing since midwinter when they sensed the lengthening daylight. Experiments with birds prove that the longer days of spring trigger change in wintering birds. Birds become rest-

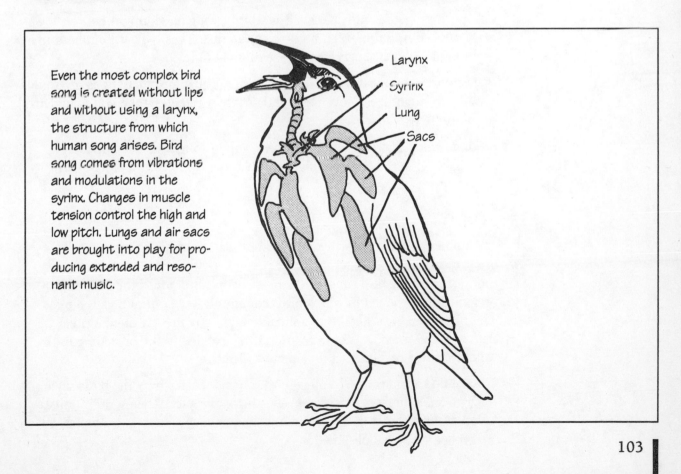

Even the most complex bird song is created without lips and without using a larynx, the structure from which human song arises. Bird song comes from vibrations and modulations in the syrinx. Changes in muscle tension control the high and low pitch. Lungs and air sacs are brought into play for producing extended and resonant music.

Larynx
Syrinx
Lung
Sacs

less and aggressive, flocks break up, and the birds disperse to find and fight over territories with food and nesting sites.

Although the courtship of some birds, such as ducks and geese, may begin before the nesting territories are definite, careful observers have seen that most female songbirds choose their mates only after the males have secured territories. The largest territories are "owned" by the strongest males—those able to drive off other males with vigorous singing and chasing. Birds don't often come to blows. The carrying power of their songs lets other birds know that the singer is ready to fight if he must. Although many bird songs sound beautifully musical to our ears, the message the birds hear is probably something like "Get outa my yard, or else!"

Besides singing to establish a territory or to attract a mate, birds communicate with each other for other reasons. Each bird species has a distinct series of calls in addition to its songs. These calls give the impression of being similar to language. They are shorter, more wordlike sounds and are often directed to a specific bird or other animal.

Birdwatchers listen for certain calls that seem to express certain meanings.

- Birds in a flock may chirp and call intermittently as they feed together or fly through the night.

- Raucous warning calls alert the whole neighborhood to the presence of a snake, an owl, or a prowling cat.

- A more dangerous intruder such as a bird-eating hawk might be announced by a thin, high note—a sound that is easily heard but hard to pinpoint. At once, birds hearing the call will hide.

- Subdued, clucking calls are used by a parent quail or pheasant as its family walks through dense cover. A slightly sharper call alerts the young to danger and they scatter.

- For a few days after leaving their nest, young songbirds keep up a high, loud, begging call that gets higher and louder every time a parent with food approaches.

TO DO

The following activities will enhance appreciation of the songs and calls of birds. Quiet, outdoor listening and a portable tape recorder are your best tools for studying bird sounds. There are many situations other than those previously mentioned in which birds communicate. Communication may occur between birds and other animals, and it may involve signals other than voices. More forms of expression can be added to the preceding list by watching any birds interact for a period of time.

- Make up cartoons using known bird songs or calls. Draw the birds saying whatever sounds they make (quack, chirp, caw, etc.); then write a translation of what that might mean in human language. The best examples will be based on actual observations.

- Keep track of the times of day that birds sing the most by counting songs for fifteen minutes in the morning, at noon, and during the evening of several days. Does the number or duration of songs change a week or a month later?

- In what habitat is the greatest variety of birds heard singing? In what habitat do the loudest birds sing? Using a portable tape recorder, record passages of loud and soft music or whistling and play them in different habitats at various distances from your observation point. (Note: Do not repeatedly do this where birds are nesting.) Which sounds carry better in the woods? In the open?

- Observe the movements of an actively singing bird. Try to figure out the boundaries of its territory by mapping all of its singing positions. Do other birds of its species sing near it? Do they respond to each other in any way? If you notice a difference in the song quality that depends on the direction the singer is facing, note the direction the bird faces at various singing perches within the territory.

The calling back and forth of crows gives an impression of a developed language. Researchers have found that crows from different parts of the country respond appropriately to each other's alarm calls. Recordings of other calls get mixed responses—it seems as though crows have dialects for local or nonessential information.

TO THINK ABOUT

There is no doubt that birds are communicating with their voices, but is this communication the same as human speech? Discuss with the children the distinctions they can make between bird talk and people talk. If they have heard birds trained to say words, discuss whether the birds seemed to be truly communicating. Parrots are trained to say words by repeating certain words again and again, with rewards of food or attention when the word is said properly. People who live with parrots say that the birds also pick up phrases they overhear; they may learn to call a dog or a child's name by hearing the calls of people. What makes parrots such good talkers? One idea is that because parrots often live in the dense foliage of jungle habitats, the ability to add original sounds to their calls helps the flock or pair recognize each other and keep in touch.

 TO WATCH FOR

Watch for singing behaviors—do birds sing more in the morning than in the evening? Is the song different in any way? (Longer songs? Longer intervals between songs?)

Courtship Rituals

All animals have gestures that communicate a lack of aggression toward others of their species. Humans have them, too; we call them good manners. Discuss the possible meanings behind the manners we learn. Handshakes, waves, smiles, and hugs all show good will: "My hand is open . . . I am unarmed . . . I will do you no harm." A nod of the head, a curtsy, a bow, or, in some cultures, a tipped or removed hat all show a willingness to be humble or subordinate. Even good table manners are a demonstration of constraint and generosity, as we politely share our food.

For birds, however, life is never easy, and good manners, therefore, may not enhance survival. Food, especially, is never assured. A bird's ability to be "rude" and to drive other birds from a territory with a food source may be its only means of staying alive. Appearing big, sounding strong, and using bill and wings to frighten competitors are daily requirements for survival. Even among birds that flock together, there is constant jostling and argument as stronger birds oust underlings from choice feeding sites.

For two individuals to be able to come together, mate, and cooperatively raise young, the natural aggression that helps them survive must be turned aside for a time. In fact, in many courtship displays sharp bills are repeatedly turned away in ritual gestures, and heads bob or bow submissively. The male strives to stay near the female, but the pursuit is often tentative. At close range, birdwatchers may see that colorful or contrasting feather patterns are sometimes displayed by these movements, highlighting the gestures of the courting birds. Rhythmic phrases that are sung, hammered with a bill, or sounded with wing feathers attract females and alert other males over a distance. Whether fancy or subtle, the courting displays of each species serve to communicate the strength and health of the ready-to-breed male.

Bill touching is a common courtship gesture, even among birds that do not feed their young or their mates, such as these Canada geese.

Aggressive defense of a nesting territory is also a major activity of many breeding males. A male might easily mistake a female for another male and try to drive her away. On approaching a prospective mate, the female crouches, flutters her wings, begs for food, and gives calls similar to those of a fledgling. All are behaviors that seem to elicit the male's care-giving behaviors and turn aside his aggressive drive. As the courtship continues and the birds become familiar with each other, the dramatic rituals decrease in frequency.

TO WATCH FOR

Feeding stations—places where birds gather to feed—are good places to watch for aggressive interactions and, in spring, preliminary courtship among wintering birds, such as a male following a female or a male feeding a female. Observe birds at a feeding station over a period of several days and watch for these types of interaction.

Aggressive Interactions

- Keep a list of species able to displace other species at feeding sites.

- Observe food squabbles among the same species. Keep track of color and/or size differences between winners and losers. Males are often larger or darker or have more contrasting color patterns than females. What actions do the aggressors use to get their way?

The woodcock is normally sly and obscure, but the male's spring courtship flight is a stellar performance. Just as the first stars appear in the evening sky, the male's short call begins from the dark ground. The bird begins to fly in a wide spiral, more easily heard than seen by following the whistling sound of his wing feathers. At the top of his spiral, known only by a sound of rapid fluttering and twittering, the male sails silently to earth. On moonlit nights, the calling and spiraling go on through the night.

- If a bird stands its ground and refuses to leave, what behaviors might it use to call the aggressor's bluff?

Courtship Rituals

- Try to pick out courtship behaviors. These are often the opposite of aggressive behavior. An aggressor may make itself look taller and fluffier, or it may move directly toward another bird in a compressed, arrowlike posture. A courting bird crouches, sidles, flutters, or turns its sharp bill aside.

- Keep track of the kinds of appeasement or courtship behavior seen around a feeder from midwinter through spring. Look for one bird begging from or feeding another bird. Listen for exchanged song phrases (chickadees) and subsequent behavior in eager suitors.

Sexual Reproduction in Birds

Birds make easy subjects for initiating discussions about sexual reproduction. The elements of courtship and pair bonding feel familiarly human, while bird anatomical equipment is sufficiently different from human that the discussion doesn't get sideswiped by nervous silliness.

The procedure is simple and brief. For eggs to be fertile, that is, able to grow, the sperm cells of the male must be inserted into the female's oviduct, or egg tube. The opening for the sperm tube or the egg tube is located just below the tail feathers (the same opening where droppings leave the bird's body). For the sperm to be transferred, the female must be willing to let the male crouch on her back. In this position, the two birds turn their tail feathers aside so that their openings touch. Then the sperm are quickly ejected into the oviduct through which they swim to the area where the yolks, or ova, first enter the egg tube. Fertilization occurs when the sperm cell, containing the genetic description from the male, combines with the yolk and its genetic information. The recombination of those genes will create a new individual with a mixture of characteristics from both parents.

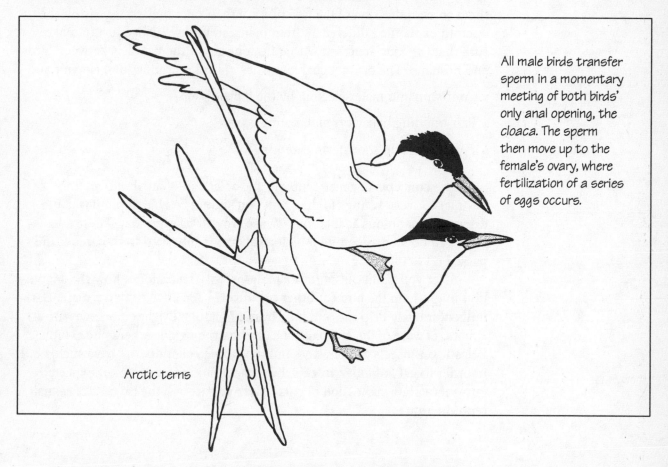

All male birds transfer sperm in a momentary meeting of both birds' only anal opening, the cloaca. The sperm then move up to the female's ovary, where fertilization of a series of eggs occurs.

Arctic terns

The mixing of same-species gene sets to make new individuals is the basis of evolution. In nonsexual reproduction (common in insects and plants), new individuals are made by an unmated parent; all offspring exactly resemble the parent. Bulblets of a garlic plant, a grove of aspen trees formed by root suckers, and the explosion of aphids on a houseplant are all examples of successful reproduction without mating. Although nonsexual reproduction works to colonize a rich habitat, any disease that brings down one member of the species will bring down all members. A population of individuals created by *sexual* reproduction, however, will have a diverse genetic makeup resulting from the combination of two sets of genes. The combination of genes from the two parents often result in variety among the offspring. A disease or naturally occurring change in the environment will affect different members of this diverse population in different ways, but chances are that even in difficult circumstances some individuals will live to breed. The sexual mixing of genes, then, may help only some individuals, but they will keep the species viable.

TO THINK ABOUT

A discussion of sexual reproduction usually includes two topics: (1) the physical act of copulation and (2) genetic mixing as a basis for evolutionary change. The physical activity is especially interesting to children as it gives them some indication of the functions of their own bodies. If possible, be open to explaining differences in human and bird sexuality, just to make sure that the kids aren't left with questions about the parallels between birds and humans. The distinct characteristics of bird reproduction behavior are:

- Courtship and mate selection by the female

- Pair-bonding behaviors and mating

- Egg-laying and short-term parenting

The concepts of genetic mixing and selection of attributes are too abstract for very young children, but you should be able to point out and discuss the fabulous adaptations we see around us every day. These adaptations can be seen as common biological events inherited from parents and passed on to offspring.

After you point out some adaptations, ask the children how the adaptation might help the bird (or other organism) keep alive or find a mate. Dark, dull colors may help the bird hide from predators. Bright colors may attract a mate. Beware of the language of causality: the woodpecker's chisel bill helps it get insects out of wood, but the woodpecker doesn't have such a bill in order to get at hidden insects. Every adaptation is a sort of unexpected gift—actually, a succession of gifts—derived through the process of sexual reproduction.

Feeding Behaviors

Each species of bird is so specialized in its feeding methods that often just a glimpse of the feeding bird is enough for identification. Most birds are easiest to see when they are feeding. If the movements can be seen by people, however, they can also be seen by predators. While feeding, a bird is in danger.

The feeding patterns of birds often appear to be resolutions to the conflict of needing to eat and needing to hide. Birds that feed in open areas such as fields or shores tend to feed in flocks, especially when not actively breeding. Flocking provides many eyes to watch for danger, and the movements of a number of birds may help confuse an attacking predator just long enough for all to escape. It also reduces the odds that any *one* individual will be taken. Birds that feed by themselves show alternating patterns of watching for predators and searching for food. The rhythm of the bird's feeding and watching are good clues for identification:

- The American robin typically feeds by running forward a short distance, stopping upright for several seconds, then repeating the sequence.

- The Northern mockingbird moves across a lawn in a similar rhythm, but may periodically extend its wings in a jerky windmill motion, revealing and concealing the white patch on its wing feathers. The flash of white may startle insect prey to jump into view.

- Birds in the flycatcher family typically sit on a perch with a view of an open area, quietly watching for insects. When an insect is spotted, the bird flies out to catch it in the air, then usually returns to the perch.

- Bluebirds feed in a manner similar to flycatchers, but their flight is heavier; they are more likely to glide toward the insect prey instead of using the swooping and fluttering wing beats of flycatchers.

Specialized feeding actions can sometimes indicate a specialized food preference or a specific use of a habitat. It's somewhat like deciding to only eat fast-food hamburgers. When hungry, you would only have to look for the familiar restaurant signs, and you would never have to compete with other feeders in line at the pizza place. To save time and energy, you'd probably begin to hang around the areas that had the most hamburger restaurants. The benefit of specialized feeding is evident in a flock of shorebirds. If several species are present in a given shore area, you can see that different feeding behaviors give different species access to food in various layers. The longer-billed birds probe deeply, the medium-billed birds sift through the upper layers, and the short-billed birds snap at visible food items. The shorebird interactions are very different from the interactions of a flock of pigeons feeding in a small area of a park. The competition between individual pigeons is intense: dominant birds try to grab food from underlings, and all birds rush to claim every new bit of food.

Feeding behavior that reduces conflict allows more energy for hunting. For foraging birds, especially mated pairs of the same species, less fighting means increased food for themselves and their young. It has been observed that male and female downy woodpeckers feed differently, even when on the same tree. The male is more likely to chisel into the wood while the female is more likely to chip off loose bark. Researchers have also observed that warblers that may live together while raising a family are likely to use different habitats when they migrate to Central America. During the winter months, male warblers are more likely to be found in mature forest settings, and females of the same species are found predominately in the second-growth scrub areas.

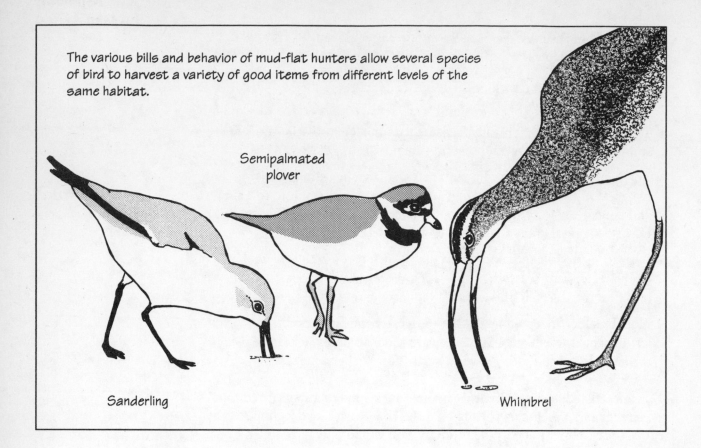

The various bills and behavior of mud-flat hunters allow several species of bird to harvest a variety of good items from different levels of the same habitat.

Semipalmated plover

Sanderling

Whimbrel

 TO WATCH FOR

Diverse feeding behaviors can be easily observed at certain times of the year. In the winter months, observe places where concentrated food sources are available—specifically at feeding stations. (Note which seeds are chosen by which species. If one seed seems to attract a variety of birds, put that seed in a variety of places and see if the bird species have preferences for feeding locales.) In the late summer and fall, when groups of different migrating species band together, diverse feeding behaviors can be observed as birds drift southward. (Most commonly, a quiet observer will first hear the sound of chickadees approaching. As the birds come nearer, other species can be seen: nuthatches, downy woodpeckers, several species of warblers, and perhaps a thrush. In the quiet that remains after the flock moves on, the careful observer might recall that each species had its own feeding territory within the dynamics of the flock. On the bark of the tree, for instance, the black and white warblers circled the branches as the nuthatches checked hiding places as they walked downward, and the woodpeckers hitched their way upward.)

 TO DO

- Set up a hunt-and-seek game in which each player works against a time limit to collect a number of scattered items meant to represent foods. The items can be small foods such as popcorn or bean sprouts (which can be eaten or composted) or small bits of plastic or paper (which must be retrieved). In nature, most birds do not try to get as many items as possible; they hunt only long enough to find a certain amount to eat. Scatter the items throughout an area and allow a few minutes to practice. Then begin the game, allowing all players the same amount of time. Set a limit to the number of items needed to make a "meal." Players who catch their fill ahead of time are Superbirds, with extra time to relax and preen. Discuss how these rules are similar to the conditions experienced by birds in the wild. What conditions in your food site made it difficult to find the food? What adaptations in a bird's body or behavior can the players imagine that would make those conditions less difficult?

■ If possible, give the players materials to "evolve" (devise, really) a Bird Tool that would make food collection easier. You might start with basic bill material (a pair of chopsticks or two popsicle sticks) and let the players create adaptations with tape, pipecleaners, or other materials. Encourage team efforts. The sharing of beneficial adaptations with others, their offspring, is a rule of life. As new ideas are tried out and evaluated, discuss the analogous trials of each generation of birds as predators and disease eliminate those "tools" that don't work well enough. Point out how the children are getting better at using their tools, just as the birds might. Try out other foods, play in different habitats, and evolve other characteristics to go with the specialized tools.

The Effects of Habitats on Birds

The habitat is the home of the bird that lives there. Birds will search until they find just the right habitat, and each species has different requirements: the kinds and density of plants must feel right for the bird's way of hiding, hunting, and nesting, and the energy the bird must use in that habitat to find its food (and defend it from other birds) must be replaced by the energy the bird gains by eating the food of the habitat. Without the right food and shelter, a tired and hungry bird soon dies.

TO DO

To develop a feeling for the qualities of various environments, develop a "Bird-Perfect Real Estate Agency Questionnaire" for the requirements of a specific bird. If the bird is well known, list its requirements, then survey and evaluate the suitability of several habitats. If a knowledge of birds and habitats is limited, the participants can first investigate several mini-habitats and then imagine birds that might use them. Using an imaginary bird frees children from the pressure of getting the "right" answer but still requires that they think about the relationship between birds and the places they live. Have the wording of the survey questions come from the children (small groups work well), but make sure that their survey acknowledges the following relationships of the bird to its habitat and the effect of the habitat on the bird's ability to hunt, nest, and rear young safely and successfully.

The large eyes of this young
wood thrush are well suited
for life in the deep shade.
Wood thrushes nest in dense
eastern woodland and win-
ter in tropical rainforest.

The survey might include these questions about the habitat:

- What is there for a bird to eat? (No North American birds eat leaves or
  wood.)

- Is there a place for a nest, a night roost, or protection from predators?

- What aspects will change when the seasons change?

The survey might include these questions about the bird:

- How does the bird's bill (or feet, eyes, hearing, or wings) help it get food?

- How does the bird escape predators?

- How does the bird keep other birds away from its food?

- How does the bird attract a mate?

- How will the young be cared for?

- Does the bird use the same habitat all year long?

When summers are especially dry in California's arid grasslands, some annual plants produce chemicals that act, when eaten, to reduce the clutch sizes of the California quail. When rains create luxuriant growth, more quail young are born.

Have the children become involved with the habitat areas they are investigating. Direct handling makes for greater knowledge. Tools help. Provide digging tools, thermometers, measuring tapes, light meters, sketchbooks, hand lenses, and containers for collecting specimens (only collect dead or returnable items). Displays for comparing the habitats can be created. Include samples of plants, charts showing ranges of light, plant sizes, insect or seed availability, soil conditions, or seasonal changes. (A display of changes that might take place in one week during leaf fall, spring weather, or before and after a rain can be dramatic.)

TO THINK ABOUT

How might the environment be different in several years? Are there young plants growing that might become large enough to shade the plants already there? Would the lives of the real or imaginary birds be changed? Is there another similar habitat where they could go? What could be done to keep the habitat just as it is? What would it take to recreate that particular habitat in another place or in a zoo setting?

TO WATCH FOR

The way a bird moves often correlates with the character of its habitat. A sandpiper, for example, would have a hard time finding insects in a treetop—it couldn't move in the right way. Look for ways in which a bird's behavior fits its habitat.

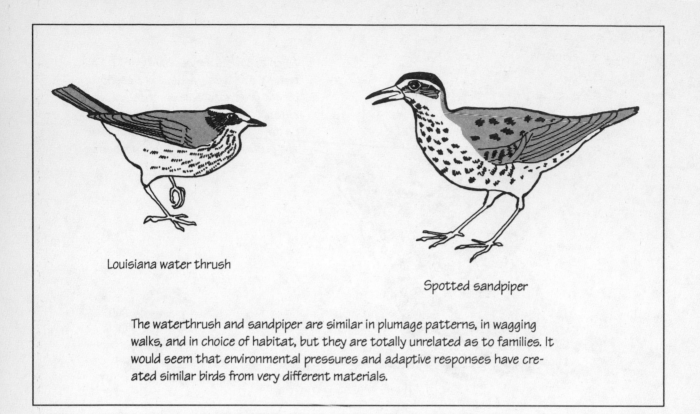

Louisiana water thrush

Spotted sandpiper

The waterthrush and sandpiper are similar in plumage patterns, in wagging walks, and in choice of habitat, but they are totally unrelated as to families. It would seem that environmental pressures and adaptive responses have created similar birds from very different materials.

Living with Predators

Humans are very blasé creatures. We enter a field or a woodland with concern only for our footing or the ferocity of the mosquitoes. Any bird would be more watchful. A bird that is not watchful will not live long. From the sky may come a hawk, in the grass may lie a snake, from the bushes may pounce a fox or cat.

We can gain some empathy for the life of a bird by being watchful when walking outdoors. Before entering a field or woods, slow down. Listen. Watch. If there are bird calls, do they express alarm? If you see birds, are they dangerous to smaller birds? Are any birds moving as if they are frightened? How would the observation of the behaviors of birds be helpful to a hunting human or other animal? How might a predator of birds behave? Which environment indicates danger: a silent one or one in which you can hear birds calling while feeding? How might a small bird enter a field? Pretend that you are a small bird and act out your behavior. Would you act differently if you were part of a flock?

The flip side of the watching-for-danger behavior of the bird is the looking-for-supper behavior of the predator. What is it like for a hawk to find and catch a wary prey? Pretend to be a hungry hawk. How will you act while hunting? (Different hawks have different techniques.) Choose a place to sit that commands a view of an area where birds might be. What prey behavior would a hawk wait for before attacking? What would be danger to a hawk?

Hawk shapes distinguish methods of hunting in different habitats. The broad-winged hawk sails in circles over open fields; the rounded wings and long rudder tail help the Cooper's hawk maneuver through the woods; and the dive-bombing peregrine can attack with great speed from high above the open tundra and prairies.

 TO DO

- The game of hide-and-seek remodeled on a predator-and-prey theme gives some sense of the need for awareness in the wild. The "sparrows" are given a short time to hide, and then the "hawk" goes searching. With one tag from the hawk's "talon," the sparrow is out of play. If a sparrow manages to make it to the hawk's nest before being tagged, it is safe. (In fact, many predators will not attack prey animals in the vicinity of their nest or lair. This innate inhibition probably keeps the predator's young from being mistaken for food.) When a set number (perhaps half) of the sparrows reach the nest, the game begins with a new hawk. Discuss techniques that either bird might use for success in this game and compare them with observations made from watching actual birds.

- Sparrow-Seek: All can be hawks and all can be sparrows in the following game. Each player copies a simple outline of a sparrow on stiff paper. Cut out and camouflage the sparrow, using colors that match a given habitat where the Sparrow-seek will be played. Each sparrow maker chooses a good hiding place (not covered) for his or her creation. When all sparrows are hidden, the players turn into hawks and go about "bagging" sparrows by writing down the location of each find. Discuss the results. Which colors and which locations provided the best concealment? Did any hawking behaviors lead to greater success (including watching other hawks)? Play the game again, if possible, to "evolve" improved hiding and seeking adaptations.

Territories

The understanding that birds sing to defend territories is a relatively recent idea. The literature of the 1800s is full of allusions to birds' songs as joyful and carefree. It was difficult for people to think of birds as singing for any reasons different from human reasons. The ways people outlined a territory with fences, markers, and maps didn't seem at all similar to bird behavior. People must have noticed that nesting birds drove predators away, but no one asked, "How far away?"

Uncovering the phenomenon of territoriality in birds required a great deal of careful observation. In a given area, all the birds of the same species were watched in turn. Their movements were mapped and recorded, especially their interactions with others of their species. Territorial behavior in most common songbirds showed a similar pattern.

It was noticed, for instance, that winter behavior patterns changed early in the breeding season. The local, nonmigratory winter flocks broke up, as the migrating birds began to fly back to breeding areas. In most cases, the males arrived first. They immediately showed aggressive behavior to other male birds of the same species (and to other females, except for the female being courted). Female birds also took part in defending territories by singing or chasing intruding birds.

Singing and/or other obvious displays were given by a defending male at several sites in a given area. The sites or perches gave a general idea of the size

Various owls and hawks may live in the same habitat, but by hunting at different times of the day and using different techniques, they avoid direct competition for available prey animals.

of the territory. More specific but sometimes changing boundaries could be identified by the interactions of two male birds. In defense of what he considered to be his territory, a male aggressively challenged and chased an intruding male. Once the chaser and intruder passed over the boundary into the intruder's territory, the chaser became less aggressive, the tables turned, and the intruder became the chaser. This behavior continued until a balance of power was reached. At the place where neither bird chased and neither fled, the boundary between the two territories was defined. Borders were sometimes defined by abrupt changes in habitat (streams, edges of fields, etc.).

In some circumstances, the mutual boundary could alter; a stronger bird might chase off a younger male or the defending male might die. For the most part, boundaries were maintained by the presence of the resident male, whose existence was announced mostly by his singing. By singing instead of fighting, the energy of the male could be turned to getting food for the incubating mate and later for the young. Singing and territorial displays usually diminished as the nestlings became independent. Renewed singing usually meant a second brood was on the way.

TO WATCH FOR

Observations of singing birds during spring and summer should show some of the behaviors discussed in the preceding paragraphs. Not all species act exactly this way, but the sequence is similar enough that some of these behaviors should be recognizable. If you can, compare the lengths of time a

Red-winged blackbird

Wood thrush

As you listen to bird songs, try out this theory: There seems to be some correlation between male fidelity and the song of the male. Males that tend to one mate and family have melodious songs; polygamous males that keep a territory for the raising of several families by several females have lower, buzzier songs.

bird sings or displays over a period of several weeks; you should be able to record a changing pattern. By correlating the singing with nest-building or food-carrying activities, you may also discover the breeding cycle.

TO DO

It is very interesting to choose a portion of a park or backyard as a personal territory as if you were a small bird. Before you choose, decide on the attributes of an ideal territory. What needs would a bird have? Think of features that support life as well as provide cover, nesting sites, and display areas. Even within a school building or playground, individuals within a group will choose different areas as their territories. Decide on how the boundaries will be marked and maintained. Keep in mind that bird songs define territories and attract mates without causing harm to other birds. If possible, try this activity in a variety of habitats. The choice of a territory (and perhaps the construction of a shelter or blind) might be used as a preliminary step for other activities such as journal-keeping, sketching, or bird counting.

Seasonal Behaviors

What differences do the seasons make in our behavior? Do we dress differently? Spend more time in some environments than others? Eat different foods? Feel differently? Help the children make distinctions between behaviors that are imposed upon them (school or camp) and those that they choose because of seasonal conditions. Which conditions influence their choices? Temperature will probably be the major influence. List together some temperature-related activities: snow play, gardening, swimming.

Birds respond to seasonal changes in ways similar to those of people. When chilly, a bird "thickens" its body covering by fluffing up its feathers. When hot, a bird will increase its heat loss by flattening its feathers, "thinning" its outfit. Open-beaked panting also helps cool down the bird. Whether a bird eats seeds or insects or preys on larger animals, it must adjust its feeding activities to seasonal fluctuations in food. For instance, the route a migrating bird takes may be relative to the bird's pattern of building up a layer of fat prior to any long-distance portions of the journey.

Birds prepare for migration and begin their trek long before temperature changes force them to go. Even first-year birds who have never experienced the effects of winter cold are usually well on their way south while food is still abundant on their home grounds. Humans, however, don't seem to have an innately strong urge to do certain activities at certain times. Our seasonal patterns of behavior are learned. We have all learned to enjoy certain activities at special times of the day or season and may feel especially lively as that time approaches. Some people have learned to wake at the same time every morning. If any of the children have experienced waking at the "wrong" time on a trip to a different time zone, they may have some understanding of how an internal clock may be set by repeated action.

The seasonal clock inside a bird seems to be innate; it is as much a part of its life as a bill or a wing. In some birds, the seasonal clock is so strong that they attempt to migrate even when raised and kept in a room with no changes in temperature or light. For most species, changes in day length (the shortening in fall and the lengthening in spring) create the need to migrate. The difference in light is perceived by their eyes, of course, but the signal is "felt" throughout the body of the bird. As the spring days lengthen, the amounts of hormones in the blood increase. These chemical messages create or amplify reproductive behaviors and signal the start of migration. One scientific study showed that when certain birds were kept in reverse sequences of seasonal lighting, they reversed the seasonal behaviors of wild birds. Under constant light conditions, they stayed in their winter mode.

By fluffing its contour feathers, a black-capped chickadee can trap a layer of insulating air, creating a heat-retaining down jacket for cold winter mornings. (Note tail feathers bent from spending the night in a tree cavity with other chickadees.)

In hot weather, the feathers are sleeked flat and wings may be lowered to help body heat escape. A bird will often pant to help air-cool its body.

TO WATCH FOR

In the months on either side of the spring equinox (about March 21) and the fall equinox (about September 23), keep records of behaviors of birds around a feeder. Watch flocks of starlings or house sparrows also. Look for changes in aggressive postures, pairing behaviors (closer following, courtship feeding, chasing of birds that approach a mate), plumage coloring, and the forming or breaking up of a flock.

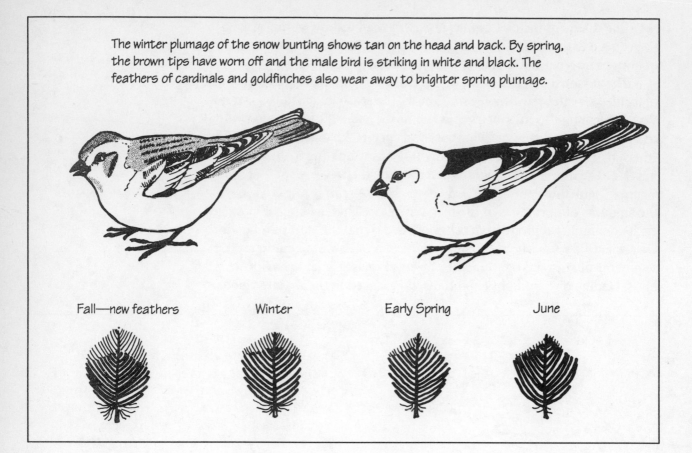

The winter plumage of the snow bunting shows tan on the head and back. By spring, the brown tips have worn off and the male bird is striking in white and black. The feathers of cardinals and goldfinches also wear away to brighter spring plumage.

Fall—new feathers   Winter   Early Spring   June

Migratory Birds

Find out if the children are familiar with the idea that birds fly south for the winter. If so, ask them why the birds migrate. After all, the journey is dangerous for the birds. They must pass through areas where their kind of food is scarce, into unfamiliar landscapes with unknown predators. Many must pass over the open ocean, with no place to land. Thousands of migrating birds are killed when they fly into skyscrapers, even if the windows are lit. Most people would mention the warmth and the availability of food as reasons. Can the children think of other reasons?

Ask if all birds fly to the same place. Many birds (herons, ospreys, hawks, geese, ducks, robins, redwings, and grackles) fly just to the southern swamps and seacoasts, where habitats are varied and food is abundant. Many of our smallest birds fly the greatest distances. The tiny ruby-throated hummingbird buzzes all the way across the Gulf of Mexico to Central and South America (and back). Most of our warblers, vireos, wrens, flycatchers, tanagers, and orioles find their way to the tropical forests of Central America where they resume hunting for insects and fruit in the leafy trees. In fact, it is probably closer to the truth to think of these birds as tropical species that "vacation" in North America, instead of the other way around. Many shorebirds, especially plovers and sandpipers, fly to South America over long stretches of water where they cannot land.

The majority of migratory birds are predators, which means that they hunt for live prey. Their prey may be insects, worms, or crustaceans, but since the food must be alive, the birds must go to habitats that never freeze. Seed-eating birds are not so pressured to migrate great distances. Migratory sparrows may be the last to leave and the first to return. Many sparrows and juncos that summer in Canada only go south as far as the northern United States. Other northern species, especially the finches and snowy owls, migrate south only during winters when food supplies are limited in their local areas.

It is thought that the diagonal flight pattern assumed by ducks and geese during extended flights creates an air flow that adds lift and reduces drag on all but the lead bird.

Even the birds that we think of as year-round residents may migrate several states south in the winter. We may not be aware of their disappearance since their places may be taken by others of the same species from several states north of us.

Our awareness of the movements of birds is largely the result of banding operations. Large numbers of birds have been tagged with numbered leg bands that can identify them when they are caught or found at a later date. By keeping track of all recovered birds, bird scientists have learned which birds go where, which paths they follow, and how much time the journey takes. The study of banded birds has revealed some interesting behaviors:

- Female and young birds of some species travel farther than the males.

- Many species travel in circular loops, especially if part of their flight is over open water. They will feed along coastal areas for the first part of the journey, then take off over water for a sustained flight as they near their destination.

- Young birds may stay on the winter feeding grounds for their first season.

- Once the bird's migrational routes are established, individuals tend to return to the same places to nest and to spend the winter.

- Most migratory birds will begin their journey before food supplies run out. They take off with stored extra fat to fuel the long flights.

- The birds that fly the longest migrational routes tend to have the strongest inner maps. Young tundra-bred shorebirds make their first migration by themselves, with only instinct to guide them along routes traveled weeks earlier by their parents.

TO DO

Keep records of the dates of the first returning birds you see. The ground-feeding birds usually arrive first. Robins, red-winged blackbirds, grackles, or killdeer might be heard or seen as soon as the ground thaws in your area. If you live near the seacoast or a large river system, shorebird and waterfowl flocks might return before landbird migrants. These first birds push north-ward as soon as the weather allows, sometimes retreating if cold returns. As you get better at identifying other migrants, list their returning dates as well. An old date book, with a page for each day, will provide room for a perma-nent record that will last for years. Add first flowering dates for plants and trees in your area for a more complete record of the tide of spring return.

TO THINK ABOUT

How birds know the routes to ancestral wintering areas is still very much a mystery. Discuss with the children how the birds might know. Research is still going on to find the answers. So far, it seems as if different species use different combinations of several methods. Some birds seem to have innate maps—they just know how to go. Others are influenced by directional clues from star patterns, from bands of polarized light, from the earth's magnetic directions, or from the shapes of the land and waterways. Some birds find their way around by recognizing odors or by observing the movements of other migrating birds. It is very interesting to think about the possibilities and how each might be tested.

Birds Watching Birds

Have the children seen birds paying attention to other birds? Make a list. Think of times when birds have responded to other birds. To start, recall times when birds gathered to feed, fought over food, called a warning when a predator bird was sighted, scattered from danger, drove off competition, courted a mate, fed a nestling, or moved as part of a flock. Encourage full descriptions of the birds' behaviors. Focus the children's attention on what the birds saw or heard other birds doing. Ask how they might have influenced each other. Writing down a description of movements and behavior might help simplify the narrative. Answer these questions: (1) What was the bird doing? (2) What signals did the bird observe? and (3) What did the bird do in response? In these descriptions, encourage the children to state only what was seen. They should save their assumptions about the birds' feelings for other activities. (For instance, descriptions of the parent robin's affection for its young while feeding the begging babies might read: "Arriving with food at the edge of the nest, parent stood a moment watching the openmouthed and clamoring brood. It responded to the largest, loudest gape by pushing a worm into it.")

The big and brightly colored mouth gapes of many baby birds not only give their parents large targets, but also trigger the parents' instinct to fill the targets with food.

Birdwatchers have been noticing increasingly subtle and complicated interactions of birds responding to their observations of other birds. The following scenarios indicate that birds watch and learn from each other in many circumstances.

- In Great Britain, a species of tit (a relative of chickadees) learned how to open fresh milk containers that were delivered and left outside. This method of getting cream off the top was observed by other tits in the neighborhood. The behavior is still being mapped by observers as it spreads to nearby areas. A similar event can be seen when a new bird feeder is placed outside. More often than not, the chickadees are the first to find it, and their feeding behavior brings other species of birds to investigate.

- In the southwest, Harris's hawks hunt in family groups. The initial search is over a widespread area, but a sudden dive by any member of the group signals the rest of the family to convene to the location. The prey is chased by one hawk after another until one succeeds in bringing it down, and the food is then shared by all.

Harris's hawks often hunt in a manner similar to mammal predators, such as wolves. By taking turns at driving the prey, the prey becomes tired and is finally taken. This kind of complex social behavior may be more common in birds than was once thought.

■ In dense tropical forest, there is some indication that pairs of birds of different species map out breeding territories more in relation to each other than to the lay of the habitat. Proximity to certain neighbors seems to take priority over available habitat with no neighbor. Observers in our temperate areas have noted that neighboring birds spend considerable time just keeping track of each other. Are neighbors of other species a priority for North American birds?

TO WATCH FOR

Once a bird is identified, continue observing it to notice in what ways it might be signaling to other birds. Note any behaviors that might be responses to signals from other birds.

TO THINK ABOUT

In what ways might it be an advantage to a bird to signal danger to other birds? Talk about what has happened when one bird signals danger to others of its flock. What might be its relationship to others in the flock? Most biologists now consider an animal's altruistic behavior toward others in its family (siblings, offspring, offspring of siblings) to be a way of protecting the shared genes of the related individuals. Think also about how a flock response might protect the signaling bird.

Mourning dove

Sudden flashes of contrasting colors on wings or tail, called "banner patches," may help a species survive by startling a predator, intimidating a competitor, or signaling to other family members of danger.

Bird Behavior: Innate or Learned?

Talk with the children about instinctual behavior. Can they think of an example of such behavior? (Flying south before winter starts, making a nest, the first flight of a nestling.) With any example, ask what there is about the behavior that makes it innate rather than learned. Focus the discussion so as to encourage the development of the concept of instinct in contrast to the concept of behavior that is learned from experimenting or from watching others. The feeding behavior of just-hatched chicks is a good example. As soon as the chicks can walk, they begin to peck at small shapes on the ground. This activity seems to be instinctual or innate—the chicks are born with it. When they see a tiny seed or a bit of dirt, they peck at it. Chicks that are kept separate from adults soon learn to distinguish between specks that are food and specks that aren't, and they begin to spend more time pecking at food items. Chicks that feed in the company of adult chickens learn to peck at a greater variety of food items sooner than chicks kept by themselves. The urge to peck at specks is innate; finding out which specks are food is learned. Most of the bird behavior we see is innate, but it is refined by the experiences and learning abilities of the individual bird.

 TO WATCH FOR

Observe the behavior of young geese, ducks, or chickens and try to figure out which behaviors are learned and which are innate. If adult birds are present, do the young birds respond to their activities in any way?

Shortly after hatching, birds learn to identify and respond to their parents. If a non-parent object happens along during the brief post-hatched period, young birds will imprint on that object instead and follow it as if it were a parent.

TO DO

- Make a list of bird behaviors observed and reported (including date, location, and influencing factors). Discuss whether the behavior might be innate or learned. Be careful not to throw adult weight to any one side of a discussion. Encourage each participant to clarify his or her ideas. Lead any tangled argument into a discussion of how to set up an experiment that will provide acceptable proof to all sides.

- Check your local library for examples of experiments in bird behavior. Any college text on bird biology will have many examples, as will books written for children or adults on the lives of birds. Books by or about Niko Tinbergen or Konrad Lorentz include excellent examples of behavior studies in the field. Bring the children's attention to possible differences in the results of experimenting in the field (relatively nonintrusive) and experimenting with captive birds in a laboratory. Don't expect any solutions to this argument; those who feel for the lives of individual birds will always oppose those who want to use laboratories to control the extraneous variables of a field situation. Make sure both sides get consideration.

When offered a dummy egg, larger than their own, herring gulls will prefer to sit on the larger egg. Bird species that are subject to parasitism by cowbirds or European cuckoos will sometimes desert clutches in which the larger egg of the parasite appears.

- If the group seems to have come to a usable understanding of the distinctions between innate and learned behaviors, introduce a discussion of human activities that might be innate. This can be an especially hot topic for adolescents. If interest is high in this area, look into research being done on newborns and studies on identical twins. The ongoing studies on wild chimpanzees and gorillas also reflect our interest in ourselves. New research is being done every year, but, at least for now, there are more questions than answers in this area of study.

129

PART FIVE

PEOPLE AND BIRDS

A bird guide and binoculars are the tools of the culture of birdwatching. They are adaptations in the same ways that beaks, feet, and bodies are adaptations. They bridge the gap when your patience or experience is not enough. You will perhaps find other tools to help you become a better birder: tapes of songs, sturdy shoes, or just the right jacket. The following activities are designed to bring you the information or the intimacy with birds that you desire. Your most important lessons and ideas, however, will come from spending time outside. You will always see something, hear something, feel something totally new.

Attracting Birds to Us

Feeding the Birds

Getting the birds to come to the birdwatchers is by far the easiest way to become involved in the pleasures of watching birds. Regular feeding, especially during the winter months, can create an early familiarity with birds so that even two-year-olds can learn bird names. But like the responsibility of taking care of a pet, bird feeding should not be the full responsibility of a child. The initial investment in feeders and the ongoing costs of feed are adult responsibilities. Home feeding of wild birds is an excellent way for adults to nurture a child's interest in nature and provide opportunities for the child to teach the parents.

The following practices may be considered as sequenced steps or as descriptions of different levels of involvement. Choose the pace or level that best suits you or your group.

- *Scatter mixed seeds or cracked corn in a variety of locations.* Birds are more likely to frequent areas that are south-facing or sheltered from the wind or that provide cover. If you leave seed on a regular basis, the birds will come regularly, perhaps even learning to associate you with the appearance of the food. Choosing sites you can observe from a window will make it easier to watch for longer periods. You might start the feeding program at a distance, gradually scattering seeds closer to the observation window as the birds become familiar with the food source. If snows are deep in your area, a lean-to of boards or old Christmas trees will concentrate ground-feeding birds near you when the ground is covered.

- *Hang vertical tube feeders from branches or brackets to attract a different variety of species.* Birds that can feed on the trunks or branches of trees can easily manage the swinging feeders. The small openings on these feeders slow down the rate of feeding. One type has tiny holes for dispersal of Niger or "thistle" seed and will be used by various finches.

- Most of the native winter birds can be attracted by the combination of ground feeding and tube feeders. The consumption of seed is not overwhelming, and the equipment costs are modest. The system resembles naturally occurring feeding situations, and it is not necessary to keep food in constant supply. The addition of suet, secured by a wire screen to a branch or post, will provide food for extended periods to winter residents such as chickadees, woodpeckers, nuthatches, and titmice.

- *Put food on platforms and hopper-type feeding stations.* With more food available, you are likely to attract more birds. Be aware that you are also making food more readily available to numbers of animals you may not wish to

Feeders do not have to be fancy to attract birds and bring pleasure to the watcher. Start with your own inventions to get an idea of what works for your area's birds.

feed, including flocks of aggressive, non-native birds such as starlings. On the other hand, people don't seem to mind having their supplies wiped out by flocks of evening grosbeaks. In general, the more food you put out and the greater your constancy in providing it, the more likely you will attract birds that travel in flocks. Flocks are like committees of humans; they prefer to stick to schedules and proven procedures. If food is constantly available, a flock will be more likely to include you in their itinerary. Smaller amounts of food put out irregularly will be less likely to attract flocks of starlings, pigeons, or house sparrows.

133

Unwelcome Visitors

The food you put out will also attract a wide range of creatures you may not intend to welcome. Mice, rats, shrews, and flying squirrels may feed during the night. Red, grey, and fox squirrels, raccoons, and opposums will all try to cash in, possibly doing damage in the process. Many people are not pleased to find themselves supporting flocks of introduced birds or small wild creatures. Before beginning a feeding program, try to decide on the limits of your generosity and take steps to avoid attracting unwanted animals. Limited food is the best tactic. Use strong wire to attach all feeders. Invest in a feeder with some sort of baffle system if you wish to discourage jay-sized birds and squirrels.

If you are attracting birds, you will also be attracting animals that prey on birds. It can be infuriating for a bird lover to see a cat kill a feeding bird. Place feeders high up and away from potential predator hiding places so that cats cannot sneak up on unwary birds. (Birds tend to stay longer at feeders on second floors; perhaps they sense that they are safer there.)

Try to think about how you might feel if you happen to see a hawk "feed" on a chickadee that is at your feeder. Sharp-shinned hawks are especially well-adapted for the surprise maneuvering required in such a situation. You (and the chickadee) won't see more than a flash of dark wings. Hawks are responsible for a quick and natural end to many a small bird's life, and there are many more small birds than hawks. It is rare and special to see one in action (and illegal to attempt to harm the hawk in any way).

One way to deal with feeder problems such as squirrels, starlings, raccoons, cats, and hawks is to become interested in their behavior. Pay attention to their ways of getting food. Set problems for them and see how they solve them. What social behaviors do they display? It is not recommended that you become so friendly that you put out special food for mammals. Extra food will attract extra animals or support an increase in offspring that the natural environment cannot support. They may get accustomed to your presence and may even learn to scratch on the door when they want food, but keep in mind that these wild "pets" will not hesitate to use aggression to get food, and inexperienced children are often victims.

Varieties of Food

You might want to set up an experiment on the food preferences of different bird species. Once an initial variety of birds become regulars to your feeding area, devise an experiment in which equal amounts of different foods are available from the same type of feeding dish in the same area. Animal feed stores are likely to have supplies of unmixed seeds. Keep track of the foods that are preferred. (Take into account the relatively faster disappearance of larger portions. Bread pieces will disappear more quickly than millet seeds.) Do ground feeders have different preferences than the platform feeders? Can the rapid disappearance of some foods be accounted for by the tastes of birds that come in large flocks? Are they the birds you want to attract?

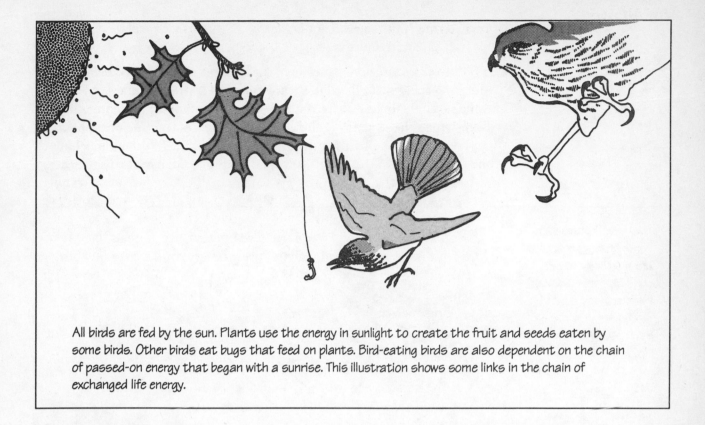

All birds are fed by the sun. Plants use the energy in sunlight to create the fruit and seeds eaten by some birds. Other birds eat bugs that feed on plants. Bird-eating birds are also dependent on the chain of passed-on energy that began with a sunrise. This illustration shows some links in the chain of exchanged life energy.

The following list gives some idea of the varieties of foods you might buy to attract birds. The first items are easiest to get and will attract the greatest variety of wild birds.

- *Mixes of seeds:* Choose mixes with higher proportions of sunflower seeds, white millet, and cracked corn. High proportions of reddish millet, wheat, and oats give mixes a darker, browner look. Native birds go for these seeds last, but they are attractive favorites of flocks of starlings, pigeons, and house sparrows.

- *Sunflower seeds:* More of the smaller, darker sunflower seeds will fit into a tube or hopper feeder. You will therefore get more feeder visits out of a bag of small seeds than you will from an equal weight of large, striped seeds. Sunflower seeds are high in fat and protein. To a bird, a diet high in sunflower seeds translates into less energy used for greater energy obtained, hence its preference among many birds. The shucked hulls can create a minor litter problem, and there is some indication that the hulls can cause dieback of lawn grasses.

- *Cracked corn:* Corn can be used as a mainstay for attracting pheasants, grouse, turkeys, or quail. It is sometimes used to lure big eaters such as squirrels, jays, or crows away from the more expensive foods.

- *Bakery products:* Bread, pastry, and doughnuts are readily eaten by birds. The smell of these goodies may also attract dogs, squirrels, raccoons, opposums, or rats, but they will not be steady customers if baked goods are put out only on an irregular basis.

- *Suet:* Suet is all fat and is valuable in supplementing the diet of many native wintering species. If offered in a firmly mounted wire container, it will be available after the seeds have run out, a consideration for those freezing dawns when the seed tray is empty. Combinations of suet and peanut butter can be made or purchased and are appreciated by bluebirds and mocking birds. Any seeds in the "cake" are superfluous and are usually discarded by suet-eating birds.

Avid suet eaters at a home feeder, chickadees are also likely to scavenge fats and protein from animals slain by predators or winterkill, such as this deer.

- *Niger seeds:* Often called "thistle seeds," these high-fat, tiny seeds are perfect substitutes for native weed seeds and are relished by all finches. A special tube feeder with appropriately tiny dispensing openings will restrict the use to only the smaller birds.
- *Melon, squash, and pumpkin seeds:* Any of these seeds make excellent bird feeds. The birds don't need them to be cleaned in any way, but you may want to put them on a separate tray or on the ground, otherwise your feeding station and the other seeds might become moldy from contact with the juices and pulp.

- *Fruit:* Various fruits can be offered to try to attract species that are not interested in seeds. The time of year and the climate of the area will affect the results. Try slices of apples and oranges, dried fruits such as raisins and currants, or collected wild fruits when available.

TO WATCH FOR

Does the weather influence feeding behavior at your feeder? If there is a forecast for colder weather or rain or snow, is there an increase in rate of feeding or visits from new species?

Creating an Environment for Birds

Whatever the size of the area you would like to make attractive to birds, several goals are common:

- Some open space (lawn or soil) for easy insect hunting

- A border of flowering and seeding nonwoody plants (annuals, perennials, and grasses) for cover and food

- A mix of deciduous and evergreen woody shrubs, providing berries, perches, nest sites, and protection from strong winds and predators.

Pay attention to the natural landscaping of areas where birds are numerous. Are the previously listed attributes present? Can you see any other relationship, element, or kinds of plants that make up a good bird habitat? Sometimes it can help to think about the characteristics of habitats where birds *don't* go. In general, any area in which all the elements are the same is not a good bird habitat. An expanse of lawn, a field, a forest of trees of the same age and species, or a beach may be visited by certain birds for feeding or even nesting, but they are more often empty. In general, the greater the variety of spaces and species of plants, the greater the variety of birds that will use an area.

The best source of ideas for landscaping arrangements and kinds of plants are the natural areas near you. Visit nature sanctuaries or wildlife preserves and find out where birds are likely to gather. Talk to the people who work in such areas. Find out the names of the plants most used by local bird populations. You may find that your ideal bird habitat would take lots of labor and money to create. You might want to start with these simple ideas for creating a more natural, diverse, and bird-oriented backyard.

- Mark out a strip for annual grasses and weeds along the border of your property. It may be the border between your lawn and your neighbor's lawn, or the area between a lawn and shrub border. Turn over the soil with a shovel or rototiller in a strip 3 feet wide. Local annual weed seeds are already in the soil, so you don't have to seed it. You (and your neighbors) might enjoy a mix of colorful flowers added for a "gardenesque" effect. Any flowers in the daisy family will be summer-long bloomers and produce seeds for birds; tall marigolds, zinnias, cosmos, coreopsis, and sunflowers will also fit well into a grassy background. You can also try a commercially prepared meadow mix. In any case, the strip of "field plants" must be rototilled or plowed under every two years to maintain a rich collection of seed-producing plants.

Hummingbirds can be attracted to a yard by planting red flowers such as geraniums, salvia, impatiens, fuchsia, or red runner beans. These blossoms become an important feature of the bird's territory, and they will vigorously defend them against visits by other hummingbirds.

- If a tree, a fence, or a building is already a part of the area, plant a mixed border of shrubs close to the larger element. Try for a sloping effect, with shorter bushes in front and larger bushes near the tree trunk or wall. When the plants grow together, they will create a bank of leafy branches, a highly attractive habitat for birds.

- Use plants and fences to create a south-facing windbreak. The warmth of the sun and protection from the wind will draw the birds to this shelter. Cast-off Christmas trees can be propped together to make a temporary winter shelter. If the ground is covered with straw or leaf litter, insects may also be attracted, providing food for foraging birds.

- Similarly, a brushpile will create an "instant shrub" that attracts denizens of the ground and brush (sparrows and towhees, thrushes and wrens). Lay down large limbs first to create open areas under the layers of interlocking branches. Branches might also be piled at the base of a tree. Tie or "plant" a

This lean-to brushpile, made to shelter birds over the winter, provided a summer nesting site for a robin family. Although it was low enough for a small child to look into it, the young were safely hatched and fledged.

sturdy limb in the area of the feeder; this will provide a resting place for birds waiting to feed (and will provide you with better views).

- Water for drinking and bathing will increase the number of birds and bird behaviors you can observe. A rough-bottomed, shallow disk (even an inverted trash can lid) will do for the container. Fresh water seems to be appreciated, and some birds are attracted to dripping water. A bucket with a small hole or a drippy hose suspended over the bathing container serve this function well.

- Look for other ideas and lists of plants in books written specifically for landscaping for birds and other wildlife. Stephen Kress's *Guide to Attracting Birds* has detailed information for creating a bird-friendly environment.

Birdhouses

Take a walk through any mature woodland and look for standing dead trees or barkless limbs. Dead wood is usually abundant in a natural habitat. It is also crucial as a source of insect prey and shelter for many of the woodland birds. You will have to look hard to find any dead wood near human neighborhoods. Without the potential nesting sites, cavity-nesting birds are not able to breed, and populations are severely limited.

In earlier times when most Americans lived in "the country" and wooden fence posts were common, bluebirds were a familiar sight. Nesting sites in the tops of rotten posts were readily available. Loss of posts, competition with house sparrows, and overexposure to pesticides have greatly

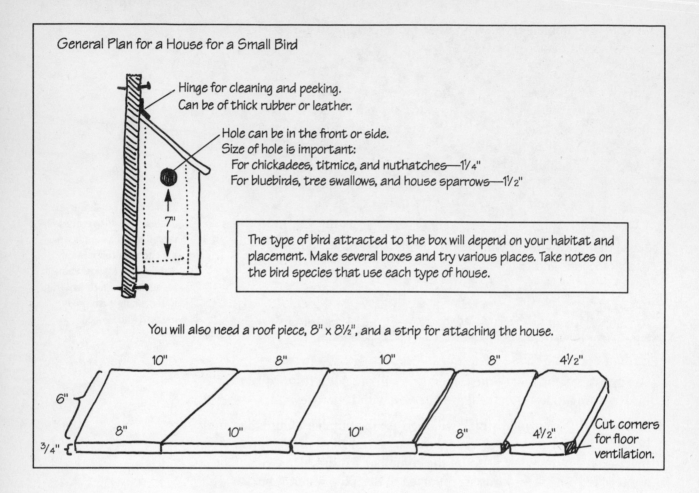

General Plan for a House for a Small Bird

Hinge for cleaning and peeking.
Can be of thick rubber or leather.

Hole can be in the front or side.
Size of hole is important:
 For chickadees, titmice, and nuthatches—1¼"
 For bluebirds, tree swallows, and house sparrows—1½"

7"

The type of bird attracted to the box will depend on your habitat and placement. Make several boxes and try various places. Take notes on the bird species that use each type of house.

You will also need a roof piece, 8" x 8½", and a strip for attaching the house.

10"   8"   10"   8"   4½"

6"

8"   10"   10"   8"   4½"

¾"

Cut corners for floor ventilation.

reduced the numbers of bluebirds. Fortunately the bird is well-loved, and many people have made efforts to provide nest boxes in protected sites. As a result, the bluebird population is now increasing.

Making a birdhouse and watching the activities of a bird family is a wonderful way to get involved in the lives of birds. The activities of the breeding pair provide examples of many bird behaviors: courtship, territory defense, nest-building, care of the young, learning behavior, and elusion of predators. People have experimented with ways to attract various species of cavity-nesting birds. Many species will be fussy about the size of the nest opening or the size of the interior space. The dimensions listed for the houses of common birds on the illustration will provide some guidelines. The following considerations are the results of many house-builders' experiments and observations:

- Inexpensive, rough-cut lumber makes the best building material. Interior-grade plywood or fiber board is more likely to warp in the rain.

- Painting the house or staining with toxic stains will undermine your efforts to provide a safe environment for baby birds. Let the wood weather naturally or preserve it with linseed oil on the outside only.

- Two species of birds may fight over one nest box (especially bluebirds and tree swallows or bluebirds and wrens); put two boxes close to one another to solve the problem. Birds tend to be more tolerant of other species than they are of same-species rivals.

■ If your hopes for attracting native birds are continually thwarted by starlings and house sparrows, consider the following ideas. Starlings cannot use a nest box with an opening less than an inch and a half across. Blocking the entrance to or removing unwanted nests in a nest box might discourage the early house-hunting of house sparrows. They also prefer close proximity to buildings. (Just remember that the opening for bluebirds *must* be an inch and a half across. Bluebirds are slightly more tolerant of open areas, so try putting the box about 25 feet from the nearest tree.)

■ Both starlings and house sparrows will prey on nestlings, at least in the sense that they will kill young birds in the process of taking over a nest box. Raccoons and cats will also destroy or disrupt the brood. Frame the opening of the nest box with ³/₄-inch strips of wood, glued or nailed to the outside of the box. This inner rim will make it more difficult for predators to reach through the hole and down into the nest. Do not put a perch outside the opening. A slick metal or plastic collar around the pole or a thick coating of engine grease will keep climbing predators, including snakes, from approaching from below. The loss of nestlings to predators may be maddening and saddening to a lover of birds. Respect for the survival abilities of the predators may help you to accept the event (and to use the experience to design a safer birdhouse).

■ Choose a site that offers a clear line of flight for the parents, facing south or away from the prevailing wind. If the side with the opening is vertical or

Birds will tolerate some snooping at their nests. Keep visits short and movements low-key. A hinged top will let you check briefly on the progression of eggs to fledglings.

facing slightly downward, chilling rain is less likely to enter the nest. Boxes mounted on poles are easier to protect from predators that climb, but nearby shrubs or trees will provide safety for the fledglings leaving the nest.

■ Read other books that discuss birdhouse construction and placement in detail. See Bibliography for suggestions.

 TO DO

When you are sure that the nestlings have left your birdhouse, remove the nest. Sort out the materials according to sources (feathers, tree twigs, yarn) and try to find out where the birds might have found each material. Did any come from outside the bird's territory?

Caged Birds

Having a bird of one's own is an attractive fantasy for many people. An affectionate pal to sit on your hand and call you by name, a friendly face among creatures that are usually preoccupied or fearful, seems like an ideal pet. But that face is more a mask. A bird is not a person, and its bird nature and needs may make the relationship undesirable after a while. Please do not consider buying a bird until you have also considered the following aspects of bird ownership:

■ Shy or nervous birds are not fun. Unless the bird comes to you when very young (just a few weeks old) or has been handled since it was young, it will probably stay too fearful to be friendly. Be aware that pet store owners will often tell you (untruthfully) that their birds are young.

■ Most of the medium-sized birds (conures, large parakeets) and some of the large parrots in pet stores are trapped in the tropics and brought to the United States, in some cases illegally. Many of the birds that are trapped die in transit. To buy a wild-trapped bird is to support the importation of tropical species, a practice that threatens the survival of individual birds and perhaps whole species. Most pet-store finches, canaries, parakeets, and cockatiels are locally bred (check to be sure), and some pet stores specialize in breeding their own birds. By dealing with a breeder, you will be supporting the effort to protect the birds, and you will be learning about your bird from a caring enthusiast.

■ At some point, your human need for variety will come up against your bird's limited learning ability. In the process of learning a few behaviors, your bird will have become dependent on your attention, but you may have become bored with its tricks. Most of the birds that can learn tricks are social creatures, usually parrot-types. If you have no time to play or talk with them, parrots are very good at devising ways to get negative attention. Loud screaming or biting are just starters. One frequently sees ads in classified sections that read: "Parrot for sale, needs attention." Make sure you consider your bird's needs as well as your own.

Parakeets can be ideal bird pets. Most individuals can be tamed by gentle handling.

- Many tropical birds are very noisy. They keep their flocks together with piercing calls that can be painful to human ears. For this reason, tropical birds are often displayed behind glass cases in the pet store. Even a parakeet on a jag can be irritating; a cockatoo can actually cause hearing loss.

- Birds also bite; any bird will bite when threatened. A curved parrot-type beak is very strong, and any bird larger than a parakeet can break the skin of a finger or ear. Purchasing a bird that has been hand-fed since babyhood reduces your chances of a painful relationship.

Although these factors are the result of actual and common negative experiences, there are also positive reasons for learning to live with a bird. The best reason may be the perspective it gives to watching wild birds. Having watched a caged bird preen or bathe or feed, you will experience the similar

143

activities of distant wild birds in greater detail. The familiar gestures are no longer obscure.

Pet owners also have a special knowledge of the individuality of their pet, which is easily transferred to a respect for individuality in wild birds. For children, this is not a minor aspect of their relationship to the natural world. The awareness of individuality in birds, trees, and habitats reflects the children's growing sense of their own differences. That connection to nature has long been a source of comfort and strength for humans.

TO DO

- Read pet care books or talk to breeders and owners to learn more about keeping a bird in a home. Look for connections between the needs of caged birds and bird behaviors in the wild.

- What are the general characteristics of birds commonly kept as pets? How might those characteristics be advantages to birds in their wild lives?

- Discuss the social or reproductive needs of caged birds. What does a breeder have to provide for birds in order to get them to court and breed successfully?

- Most bird owners will tell you that the birds are really happy in their cages and are uncomfortable when brought out. Why might that be so? Find out the precautions that must be taken before your bird can be allowed the free dom of flying outside its cage.

- Find out more about how birds learn to talk. What characteristics make birds good talkers? Try to find out about the studies done on language learning in the larger parrots.

Studying Birds in the Field

How to Bird

It's hard to imagine anyone becoming interested in birds without some guidance from another person. Friends, relatives, teachers, or characters in books or films might model the pleasures of watching birds. The involvement of a trusted person provides a direction to look and a way to act. Spending time with other birders is the fastest way to learn about birds and birding. Most of this book has been about birds and bird behavior. The rest of the book attempts to give some general guidelines about birdwatcher behavior.

Finding Birds Outside

Different habitats will be home to different kinds of birds. Areas of land that are protected by the town or state are often remarkable for their birdlife, especially wetlands or coastal areas. The greatest varieties of birds are found where habitats overlap: edges of woods, thickets or fence lines along a field, trees around a pond, or the mouth of a river.

Walking quietly is essential. Conversation will distract you and alarm the birds. Stop frequently and look around. Birds hiding nearby might become frightened and decide to fly away as you approach them. Fasten your eyes on one place in the landscape and watch for any small movements, then shift your stare to another area. Moving eyes are less likely to see moving birds. The best technique is to sit still for a length of time. Passing birds may not notice a quiet watcher and may come close by. Lie down flat or climb a tree, and birds are likely to approach just to see what you are. Edwin Teale wrote that his best birding was done from a hammock. He guessed that his horizontal position was "unhuman" and nonthreatening. Take advantage of any cover that might hide your shape from view. You might want to try building your own blind, but sitting in a rain parka often works just as well (and gives some protection from bothersome insects). You may also find that gardening provides a good opportunity to listen for birds. The main point is to be outside—a lot.

Noises That Help

Making noises that attract birds is an iffy art. A sound that brings a bird in close one time may not work at a different season. In addition, a sound that works for one bird may not work for a different bird.

The greatest variety of birds can usually be found where different habitats (here, meadow and woodland) come together. If you stand with the sun to your back, the birds in front of you cannot see your movements distinctly.

When birds are aggressively defending their territories or their young, unusual sounds are likely to attract them. Walking with a pet cat or snake during the nesting season or picking up a fallen nestling and having it protest loudly is certain to attract a bevy of mobbing birds. The effect is unnerving, however. A milder reaction of curiosity can sometimes be elicited by "squeeking" or by "spshing." Squeeking involves making high kissing sounds while holding the back of your hand partially against your lips. This "small mammal in danger" sound can bring curious birds out of the bushes. It can also attract predators of small mammals, so keep your eyes open for a fox or coyote. The "spshing" sound seems to work especially well on warblers, sparrows, vireos, and thrushes. Rapid "shhs" as though hushing someone, but with a "p" sound thrown in, can bring a late summer group of warblers closer than your binoculars can focus. Both sounds work best if you have been moving quietly and if you are partially hidden by bushes when you make the sound. The birds will have to come close to see what you are.

When to Find Birds

Birdwatching is best at certain times of the day. For instance, at the first gleam of light in the early morning, birds are out and about even though you may only hear them. Once you become familiar with bird songs, that dawn chorus on young summer mornings is a special joy. During midday the birds are less active and much harder to see or hear. Late afternoon and early evening bring another period of visible and audible activity. (Hawks might be easier to find soaring on the rising air currents at midday, and owls and whippoorwills may be obvious only at night.)

Birds are part of every season. Their behaviors, appearances, and absences create the patterned fabric of a year. Spring has its beginning in the first courtship song of a wintering bird. Summer begins with the dispersing of the winter flocks and the breeding of the paired birds. In autumn, new families blend with flocks and head southward, leaving behind a simplified cast for the winter drama. Unexpected birds can arrive at any time. You must be outside, looking around, to see them.

What to Take with You

Wear clothes that will keep you comfortable for the time of year and the habitat. If you are likely to be exposed to ticks and other insects or brush, wear long pants and long sleeves. A light jacket with pockets large enough for a bird book and a snack is often convenient. If the day is hot, the jacket can be tied around your waist. On cold days, a sweater underneath the jacket can hold in warmth. A wool hat, sweater, and mittens will provide warmth in cold rain or mist. Sunscreen plus a hat or sunglasses to protect you from bright sun will add comfort to a day spent in the open (and to the evening back home).

Field Glasses

You don't need binoculars to enjoy birds; watching birds only through field glasses can keep you from seeing the rest of the environment—the "big picture" of the bird's world. Still, binoculars are magical. They move you up close to see details you could never see without them. Include them if you can.

If you are purchasing binoculars for birdwatching, look for something lightweight. A heavy, high-power pair will be hard to hold steady. Those little guys in the treetops are hard enough to find as it is. Binoculars are usually marked with two numbers. The first number is the power of magnification. Many good birding binoculars are 7x or 8x. With binoculars of higher power you may have difficulty focusing on subjects closer than 20 feet. The second number, after the "x," measures the width of the lens at the larger end. In general, the wider the lens, the brighter the image and the larger an area you see when you look through. Most birders use 7x or 8x35 binoculars because of their versatility. Binoculars of 8x50 will bring more light and detail to your eye, but the weight and size may be uncomfortable for long use. Even so, 8x50 binoculars are the best size for scanning for birds over a distant landscape (beach, marsh, open field, or sky). You may be able to use them more comfortably if you can prop your arms on the ground or against a car.

Let children start out with good field glasses. The view through toy varieties can be so blurry that children lose interest. Pocket-size binoculars, with the strap slipped over the head and one arm, will be safe with minimum supervision.

All field glasses vary in quality. You will want a sharp image with clear colors for accurate identification. The best lenses are, of course, very expensive. Check out camera shops for good used models. When trying them out check for the following:

- Hold the glasses firmly and give them a little shake. Any rattle will mean a loose lens and fuzzy images.

- Make sure that the eyepieces can be moved to fit your eyes. If you can't change the distance between the eyepieces, you will see two circles instead of one when you look through, and you won't be able to focus properly.

- Test the sharpness of the image by focusing on a small object at least 20 feet away. Check to see if the right eyepiece moves independently; this offers you accommodation for differences in your eyes. Find the focus for the left side by covering the right lens (don't squint) and using the central focus wheel to focus. Set the right eyepiece on "0," cover the left lens, and turn the eyepiece until the image looks sharp. Use this technique for comparing several brands of binoculars in the store and outdoors, if possible.

- Check for detail of design and trueness of color by focusing on several objects at different distances. Stand looking toward a light source (or toward a sunny window) and focus on a defined edge. A fuzzy rainbow around the edge indicates blurry transmission of color. You'll need all the clear colors you can get when watching warblers in the fall. You may want to look for lenses with color coating, which protects the glass and cuts down on glare.

- Focus on the lettering of a sign or a horizontal line (overhead cable) and check the focus off to the edges of the visible circle. Is the focus still accurate for the words or lines at the far left and right of center? The image in a high-quality pair of binoculars will be sharp throughout the field of view.

- Even if you feel you can't afford them, try out the high-quality, expensive binoculars. The image might be so superior that you will think of some way to buy them (or know what to look for in sales). They are also more likely to last a long time.

Scope and Tripod

For close observation of distant shorebirds (sandpipers, ducks, herons, and others), a spotting scope is a desirable luxury. Most birders find that a magnification of 20x is most versatile and that a tripod stand is needed to steady the image. Give the tripod a trial run before you buy. Pretend that you've just spotted a peregrine falcon on the other side of the store and see if you can set up the scope before it takes off. Choose flick-lock action rather than turn-to-tighten joint locks on the legs of the tripod.

Camera

If you want to take photographs of wild birds that look like the pictures in bird books, you will need expensive and specialized equipment. If you are an amateur photographer, you should talk to experienced photographers to find out about affordable cameras and lenses. You might start out taking pictures of caged birds or birds at a window feeder just to see what kinds of images you want to capture. For experience in the field, take a camera with you one day and try getting pictures of birds in their habitat. The exercise of finding the bird and framing the picture will sharpen your awareness in new ways. The need to stalk your subject will increase your hunting skills as well. Many gun-bearing hunters have found photography to be a satisfactory substitute for collecting by killing.

Locating birds at their nests is a sure way of taking pictures of birds but presents definite dangers to both parents and young. If the nest is newly made and the eggs newly laid, the parents may be scared off by your presence. Some birds may not try to nest again, and the chance to breed in that year will be gone. If the babies are nearly ready to leave the nest, your appearance may startle them over the edge too early. You might also bring danger to the nest by attracting the sharp-eyed attention of local threats: crows, jays, cats, or cowbirds. They will be aware of your movements and will know that alarm calls mean a nest is near.

Having honestly assessed the situation and taken the preceding concerns into consideration, you may know of a nest you feel may be safely photographed. Some photographers have found that erecting a blind near the nest and leaving it there for several days gives the birds a chance to get used to "company" and allows the photographer the time to try many shots. It's been said that the birds will return to the area sooner if the photographer is

Birds that live in zoos and parks can afford some wonderful shots and opportunities to observe a variety of behaviors.

accompanied to the blind by a friend who is then seen leaving, the theory being that birds can't count and will think the interlopers are gone. You might try setting up a dummy camera made of boxes close to the nest, replacing them with your real camera when you want to take close-up photos. Be sensitive to the bird's reactions to your efforts. If they continue to scold longer than ten minutes or fail to return to eggs or nestlings for thirty minutes, you must leave. Be particularly careful not to drive off incubating adults on very hot or very cold days.

Field Notebook

Notes and sketches made while you are in the field are your most valuable records, as references for yourself and also for others. Most importantly for you, the discipline of writing and sketching will help you to look closely and notice details, thereby increasing your knowledge.

Responsibility to Other People

A great deal of birdwatching can be done from a backyard and in town parks or on state land. If you think that the land you want to walk through is privately owned, you must find the owner and ask permission. Not only will you save yourself an embarrassing confrontation when found trespassing, but the owner may know of interesting sites or nests. Many people own land for the pleasures of observing and protecting the local wildlife, and they are pleased to share information with responsible people. Once permission has been granted, let the owner know when you might be visiting and find out if he or she wants to be informed of subsequent visits.

Let each visit (on private land or public) express your respect for the land and its residents. Walk quietly, keep to paths (but stay away from private

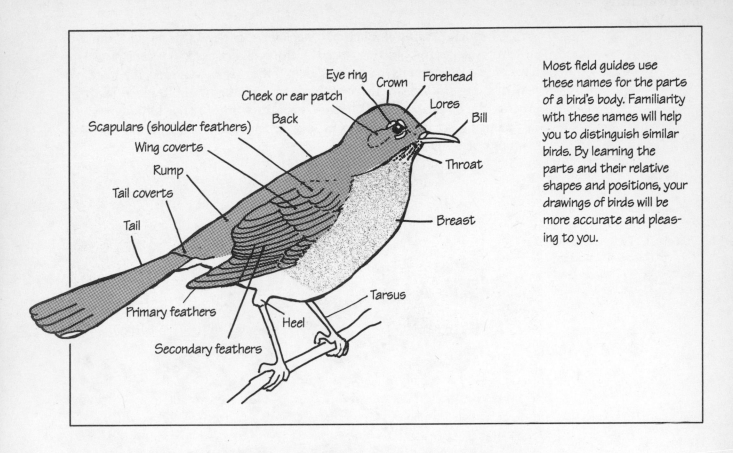

Eye ring
Crown
Forehead
Cheek or ear patch
Lores
Scapulars (shoulder feathers)
Back
Bill
Wing coverts
Throat
Rump
Tail coverts
Breast
Tail
Primary feathers
Tarsus
Heel
Secondary feathers

Most field guides use these names for the parts of a bird's body. Familiarity with these names will help you to distinguish similar birds. By learning the parts and their relative shapes and positions, your drawings of birds will be more accurate and pleasing to you.

homes), don't collect souvenirs, and always carry your trash out with you. Many landowners keep cows, sheep, or horses and may be maintaining hayfields. Close any gates, don't tromp through the hayfield, and don't bring your dog, no matter how much Puppy would love the exercise. There is a widespread cultural attitude that land without houses on it may be used by anyone in any way. This disrespect leads easily to the misuse and destruction of land meant to be kept wild by private owners and municipalities. Make sure that your actions are a model of caring behavior: you will be allowed to come again and others may learn from your good example.

Counting Birds in a Flock

Keeping track of the size of bird populations can help us tell how well the birds are doing as well as the condition of the birds' environment. Birds can't be jammed into their preferred habitat; only a certain number can find the space they need to find food for their young. If the breeding habitat is reduced, or if the area is polluted and food sources are reduced, the bird population is reduced. During migration many bird species can be counted. Large flocks can be estimated, or biologists can use nets to catch and count individuals. The results are compared from year to year.

When large flocks of waterfowl, blackbirds, or hawks are being counted, either on the ground or flying, special techniques are used. The census takers have only a few seconds to scan the flock. If they take more time, the flock may fly off or shift so that the same birds are counted twice. To speed up the process, the birds are counted in clusters of three, four, or five birds at a time. By practicing beforehand on "flocks" of seeds or small stones, the census takers train themselves to count fast.

Try counting this flock of Canada geese in clusters/multiples of three, then five. Which works best for you? Which goes faster, is the most accurate?

Adults and children can learn to take a flock census by practicing with items that are small and similar in shape. Grains of rice or soup beans are easy to handle. Begin by counting clusters of three. Groups of children may especially enjoy learning this skill. Provide challenges to individuals or teams who compete to improve their counting and multiplication skills. Use flash card flocks or known amounts of seeds shown briefly on an overhead projector. Encourage practice, as this is a skill that benefits from lots of repetition. Younger or less verbally oriented people often excel. After practicing on beans or seeds, go outdoors and try your skill on flying flocks of pigeons and starlings. Eventually it will get easier to count by groups of fifty and one hundred.

 ## TO WATCH FOR

Carefully observe a flock at rest on the ground or in trees. Can you tell by the flock behavior if there are any "watchbirds" on duty? When the whole flock takes off, do you notice any signal? As they fly, is there a leader whose behavior directs the movements of the flock? Discuss the possible clues that would signal every bird. Biologists still aren't sure of these answers. You and your observers should watch for and talk about possible communications.

Banding Birds

How can a person find out how long a bird lives? Get some ideas from the children. Possibilities might include interviewing keepers of caged birds, looking for indications of aging on a bird, or somehow marking young birds and tracking them over a period of time. Which of their ideas do the children think would work for long-term marking?

If the children seem engaged in the notion of capturing and marking birds for study purposes, follow up with some specific information. Most libraries have a book on bird banding written for children, with pictures to illustrate the process. You might decide to focus your discussion of aging and banding on a species of bird known to the children.

Before a person can trap and band birds, he or she must have a special license, obtained after proving a thorough knowledge of birds. The bander needs to know how to safely remove different kinds of birds from the trap, how to place the band on the bird, and what to write down about each bird, all without harming the bird in any way. After the bander removes the bird from the net or trap, a metal band printed with a series of numbers is carefully clamped onto each bird's leg. The numbers on the band, along with other information about the bird, is sent to an office in Pautuxent, Maryland, where the records are kept. If anyone finds the bird and sends the band to the address on the band, the records will give us some idea of how far the bird has traveled, how long it took to make the journey (if collected soon after banding), and how long that bird has lived.

Even if the birds are never found, we learn important information about birds. If a bander sets up nets or traps at the same place and for the same length of time each year, the lists of birds caught can be compared from year to year. If the birds are captured during the breeding season, the differences in kinds and numbers of birds might indicate a change in the local habitat (a field that becomes a shrubby thicket will attract different species of nesters). If the banding lists are made during migratory seasons, a change in numbers might represent a change in either the wintering habitat or the summer breeding habitat that marks the goal of the migrating flocks.

TO DO

Banding is a birding activity that definitely cannot be done by children. It is illegal to trap native birds without a banding license. Your group may be able to watch a bird-banding demonstration, however. Contact a local birding organization and ask if they know a bander who would be willing to show the children the procedures.

The process of capturing birds to be banded was made more efficient by the invention of the mist net, which allows for the safe capture and retrieval of wild birds. It still requires care and patience to release a bird safely.

Notes on Pigeons

Pigeons are the most commonly found banded bird. The bands are put on by owners of domesticated flocks bred for fancy varieties or, in the case of the stray bird, racing birds with homing instincts. It is possible to use the number on the band to find the owner of the lost bird, but you should know that the owner may not care to reclaim a bird that can't find its own way home. Also, keep in mind that bird diseases that affect humans are most likely to be found in birds that stay inside most of the year (chickens, pigeons, and caged birds), so you should not handle a tame-acting, possibly sick bird. If the bird is touched before you are aware that it may carry a contagious disease, wash your hands immediately. Later on, any containers that held the bird should be disposed of or thoroughly washed.

TO THINK ABOUT

Since bird babies have very large feet, nestlings can be banded while just a few days old without danger of outgrowing the band. That's a pretty interesting idea for us slow-growing humans: a newborn with feet the size of an adult. The smaller learners might have a good time with this idea by walking in a pair of adult's shoes for a while to see what it might be like to be a baby bird.

People-made Problems

As you talk with children about environmental problems that originate with human activities, you may run into a variety of responses. Some children simply accept the status quo: the world is as it should be; people should be allowed to do whatever they need to do. Others may be more familiar with the vocabulary of environmental concern: destruction of rain forests, pollution of wetlands, and endangerment of species might be terms they have read about or heard on television or from parents. Since children's opinions are formed by the language and attitudes they hear, your concern and involvement can give them new awareness and direction. Please be careful not to overwhelm children with feelings of despair and helplessness, even if you sometimes feel that way. (Save your strong feelings for letters to newspapers and to representatives of government and industry.) When presenting environmental concerns to children, use simple language, connect the discussion to problems they commonly see (plastic litter, for instance, which can be lethal if eaten by wildlife) and discuss possible solutions. If the children become actively concerned and want to help, ask which solution they want to work on (recycling home wastes? lobbying for local recycling projects?) and offer to help. If people are confronted with an unsolvable problem, the discouragement may cause them to turn away. Children can help. (The media is often interested in reporting children's attempts to make a difference. A positive action headed by kids can attract attention and result in beneficial change.)

The following topics can be used for discussion as you do other activities in this book or can be incorporated into a larger environmental studies curriculum. All are only brief outlines of complex and ongoing events.

Hunting

Children may initially assume that being shot at is a bird's worst problem. In fact, the majority of North American birds are protected from hunters (as are their nests and eggs). So-called game birds—ducks, geese, quail, grouse, pheasants, turkeys, and others—are protected for most of the year and are hunted only during the fall. All hunters must pay for hunting licenses, and some of the money collected is used to save land for breeding birds and to fund studies on the lives of the birds they hunt.

For the game birds, hunting poses a double threat. The birds can be killed by lead shot from a gun, or they can be poisoned by ingesting lead shot that falls to the ground. Since non-game birds and other wildlife can also be poisoned in this manner, steel shot has become mandatory in many areas. More game laws are needed to more thoroughly protect wildlife from the dangers of lead poisoning.

Attitudes Toward Birds

For much of human history, birds have been killed for food and feathers. In addition, birds that were admired in various cultures for their beauty or supposed powers have been killed to secure those attributes by magical association. Humans have always altered their environments in the process of getting meat for food and wood for shelter and fuel. But the rapid subjugation of North American wildlife and wild lands by metal machines and metal bullets has caused a phenomenal and drastic change. In one generation, huge migratory flocks of birds were eliminated forever as a result of market hunting, in which large numbers of birds were shot for commercial purposes. It was clear by the late 1800s that the destruction must be limited if birds were to survive at all. Songbirds and shorebirds were familiar market meats, and feathers were in the forefront of fashion. Wings, tails, and whole bird skins adorned hats, and hundreds of stuffed hummingbirds might be displayed as a room decoration.

During the years around the turn of this century, a movement toward bird protection began to convince people that living birds had a value of their own. Books and magazine articles alerted the public to the plight of birds, and programs in the schools taught children to care about plants and wildlife. People began to understand that crucial habitats must be set aside if the birds were to survive. Finally, laws to protect non-game birds and to limit the hunting of game birds were created after much heated public argument that even included the murder of a game warden.

TO THINK ABOUT

The issues discussed in the previous paragraphs are still being addressed today. Consider and discuss all sides of the following issues. Understanding the thoughts and feelings of each side can help to clarify the issues.

- What is the good of a bird? Should a bird be saved just because it is rare or pretty or acts nicely? Should we save ugly birds or noisy birds?

- It is against the law to capture and cage native birds unless you have a special license. How about birds from other countries? Why do people in other countries let their birds be caught and sold?

- Should land that birds can use as a habitat be taken from people who are using the land for lumbering or agriculture? Don't people have a right to make a living, too? Is it fair to limit the actions of people who live near the birds so that people far away can feel good about a saved species?

- What makes a bird common or rare? What actions can be taken to increase the number of a rare species?

- One of the lessons of the emergence of a conservation ethic in America is the power of popular opinion to change attitudes. The slaughter of birds for decoration and consumption was stopped only when it became unfashionable to kill birds. Discuss who it was who told ladies to wear egrets on their hats or consumers to eat songbirds in the first place. What attitudes or trends influence people today to continue to develop natural areas as shopping malls or to use toxic chemicals to create perfect lawns? (An evening of monitoring television programs and commercials or a perusal of magazine ads should reveal many of the attitudes that shape our culture.) How have people learned of the need to conserve? Can the effect of the influences of television, books, and magazines be heightened by your actions?

Introduced Species

Species of non-native birds have been introduced into North America since the early days of European settlement. A stubborn enthusiasm for European food, farm animals, culture, and land practices led the settlers to believe that Old World birds would be nice to have around and might even help control agricultural pests. Common around settlements in Europe, pigeons (rock doves), house sparrows, and European starlings were brought to North America and soon became common in most human environments. By the

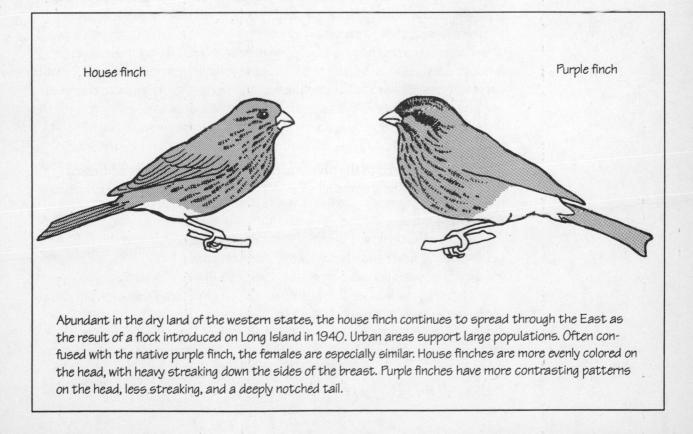

House finch

Purple finch

Abundant in the dry land of the western states, the house finch continues to spread through the East as the result of a flock introduced on Long Island in 1940. Urban areas support large populations. Often confused with the native purple finch, the females are especially similar. House finches are more evenly colored on the head, with heavy streaking down the sides of the breast. Purple finches have more contrasting patterns on the head, less streaking, and a deeply notched tail.

early decades of this century, the results of the experiments were clear: successfully introduced birds did more damage and were worse pests than any insects had been. Native birds that were able to live near people were being driven away by the more aggressive non-natives.

This story of good intentions gone awry has been repeated over and over in this and other countries. Gypsy moths that were intended to create an American silk industry destroyed our trees instead. Mongooses that were brought to human habitats to eat the snakes ate the birds instead. Goldfish released by kindhearted owners changed ponds full of clear water and abundant pond life into pools of muddy water and many goldfish. The guiding principle that explains the problem is always the same. The plants and animals of any given ecosystem are all parts of a whole. If one member is lost or if an intrusive member is imposed, then the whole is disrupted, perhaps fatally.

What sort of symbols or analogies can be used to express the concept of the balanced environment? What arguments can be put forward to dissuade an individual from introducing a non-native bird? Are there any circumstances when an introduction might be a good idea?

Pesticides

Shortly after World War II, advances in chemical technology made possible the creation of a number of very effective poisons derived from petroleum. Farmers were thrilled. The huge fields of single crops they cultivated produced large numbers of insect pests. The new pesticides effectively wiped out large populations of insects, but the effects only lasted a year or so. In many cases, a few members of a pest population proved resistant to the poison and reproduced abundantly to fill the void. Then, other new, more poisonous chemicals were created and sprayed widely.

Part of the effectiveness of these synthetic chemicals lay in their resistance to decay. Soil insects were killed for several generations. When pesticides were carried by runoff into the water systems, the immediate effects of the poisons were somewhat diluted, but small amounts were retained by water insects, which were eaten by fish, which, in turn, contaminated fish-eating birds with large doses of accumulated pesticide. Many poisoned birds died, and many others had repeated reproductive failures: eggshells were too thin, eggs didn't hatch, and hatchlings didn't survive. Despite protests of innocence from pesticide manufacturers, public outcry finally stopped the use of the worst poisons and forced studies on others. Since then, several bird populations that had been seriously threatened (the osprey and the brown pelican) have made comebacks, but not before earlier generations suffered the terrible consequences of long-lived poisons in an ecosystem.

The list of poisons still available in stores is long, and most are deadly to birds, directly or indirectly through the food chain. If you must use pesticides, try to buy those with pyrethrin (a short-lived insecticide) as a main ingredient. Compounds known as BTs are even safer because they target specific pest insects. Find out about effective methods of organic gardening, integrated pest management, and landscaping with pest-resistant native plants.

Encourage friends and neighbors to limit or stop use of chemical poisons on their lawns. If you have old, unused herbicides or pesticides stored in your house, do not throw them in the trash. They should be stored in special land-fills for toxic wastes. If your community does not have a toxic waste collection site, work to establish one.

Development of Wild Lands

Are there any areas in your neighborhood where birds are especially abundant? What is it about the property (water or kinds or sizes of plants) that might be attracting the birds? If that space became a shopping area instead of a sanctuary, where do you think the birds would go? What would happen to the birds if they couldn't find another place? As you think about this problem, keep in mind these facts about birds:

- Although some birds will spend winters in large flocks, birds are very territorial during the breeding season. One pair will chase away other birds of their own species. They seem to have an innate sense of how much hunting ground they need for an adequate supply of food. Growing babies require a great deal of food and if the parents cannot find enough food, the young may die.

- If birds cannot find territories of their own, they will not have young.

We think of birds as being extremely free. It looks as if they can take off and go any time they find a place not to their liking. We imagine that their speed in flight gives them a way to find anything they want. It is not so easy, however. Each kind of bird has very specific living requirements. Its adaptations (the way it finds food, hides, sleeps, makes a nest, and courts a mate) must fit with certain combinations of soil, water, plants, and animals. If these balanced combinations do not exist in the bird's usual habitat, the bird cannot exist.

Now, at the turn of the twentieth century, the need to save the last of our natural habitats is crucial. Most towns and cities are already beginning to develop lands that once were considered undevelopable: swamps, marshes, and edges of rivers. These areas are also the richest wildlife habitats. Get to know those lands before they are developed. Many states have conservation laws in which rare or significant wetland plants or animals are listed and under which they are protected. If the species can be proven to live or nest in the threatened area, development of the land can be halted. But first the species must be found. Knowledgable children (and adults) can stop the bulldozers effectively. Contact members of your local conservation commission for more information.

Trouble in the Tropics

During the cold and bugless winter months, many of our insect-eating birds migrate to warmer climates. It's fun to imagine them on vacation, lazily gulping bright-winged yummies in a lush tropical forest. But our fantasies are wrong—the forests are in trouble. Thousands of acres of these ancient and intricate woodlands are being cut each year. South and Central American governments see the land as being best used by people, farming is often begun as soon as the trees are cleared. Unfortunately, the rain and warmth that made the forest possible in the first place break down the nutrients in the topsoil so quickly that crops fail after a couple of years. The land is then used as pasture for beef cattle, a practice which stifles any hope of the rain forest's regrowth.

Each year the returning flocks of warblers, vireos, flycatchers, humming-birds, tanagers, thrushes, and orioles find less rain forest, less food, less shelter. It also seems to observers in this country that fewer birds come back each spring. (Indigo buntings, however, are prospering. The increased open space is just the habitat they need.)

Rather than allow all rain forests to be destroyed, some people have joined together to buy up rain forest acreage, preserving it through private ownership. Individuals or groups of children have found that they can raise money in a variety of ways and contribute to the effort to save the land. You can find out more about the issues and procedures by contacting the Audubon Society and other organizations listed under Resources (page 165).

Endangered Species

All of the problems discussed in the preceding paragraphs may contribute to the final and absolute extinction of a species of bird. This is not a distant scenario from the times of ecological ignorance such as the killing of dodos and passenger pigeons. There are birds in this country, in your state, that are presently listed as liable to become extinct. The legal term for the status of these creatures is "endangered." "Threatened" birds, plants, or animals are described as those whose existence is threatened by any further loss of habitat. "Rare" is the designation given to species that may be common in its habitat at the present time, but is at risk because the habitat is limited and any reduction would affect the population. A list of threatened and endangered plants and animals is compiled each year by the U.S. government. The list helps to mobilize efforts to save the land or create artificial breeding programs. It also adds credibility to the strong feelings of responsibility that some people have in response to the loss of variety of life forms as a result of human activities. The status of "endangered" or "threatened" does not guarantee protection—citizens and local governments must work together to enforce the laws, such as those that prohibit habitat alteration if a listed animal is present. Local awareness can be effected by individual actions. (For instance, a beach can be closed while endangered shorebirds are nesting.) The awareness can then be used to strengthen or create protective legislation. If you spot a rare species, let a local environmental group know. Birders love rare birds. If the bird stays in the habitat to breed, local attention can be drawn to the need to preserve the habitat in order to save the bird.

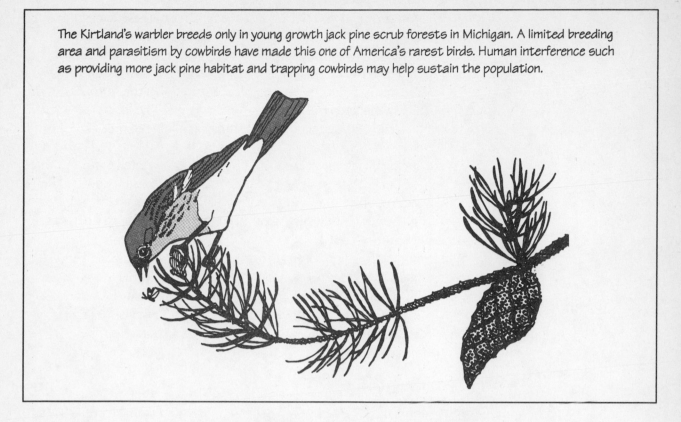

The Kirtland's warbler breeds only in young growth jack pine scrub forests in Michigan. A limited breeding area and parasitism by cowbirds have made this one of America's rarest birds. Human interference such as providing more jack pine habitat and trapping cowbirds may help sustain the population.

Even if you cannot find a bird to save, you can help by writing to legislative officials when your state or town is considering the best use of undeveloped property. Discuss all sides of the following attitudes and add your own views:

■ Why bother to save a rare bird? Animals have always become extinct: why get in the way of progress for a creature that can't make it on its own?

■ Why should wild land be left undeveloped? People need land for houses and farming. Using wild land makes jobs for people, which in turn provide clothing, food, and shelter for children. How can a rare bird be more important than human lives?

■ Do you think there should be captive breeding programs for rare birds? If there is not enough habitat to sustain a population of birds, why go to the expense and bother of keeping them alive in captivity?

If you have any trouble answering these questions or would like to hear how the pros do it, get in touch with a local environmental organization or join organizations such as the Sierra Club, The National Audubon Society, The Wilderness Society, Friends of the Earth, Nature Conservancy International, or Greenpeace. (Addresses for these and other organizations are listed in the Bibliography.)

Resources

Note: New materials are constantly being published and new groups being formed. Check your local libraries and nature book stores for updated materials and for classic oldies not mentioned here.

Books about Birds and Birdwatching

Arbib, Robert and Tony Snoper. *The Hungry Bird Book: How to Make Your Garden Their Haven on Earth.* New York: Taplinger Publishing, 1971.

Forsyth, Adrian. *The Nature of Birds.* Camden, Ontario: Camden House, 1988.

Kress, Stephen W. *The Audubon Society Handbook for Birders: A Guide to Locating, Observing, Identifying, Recording, Photographing and Studying Birds.* New York: Charles Scribner's Sons, 1981.

Kress, Stephen W. *The Audubon Society Guide to Attracting Birds.* New York: Charles Scribner's Sons, 1985.

Leahy, Christopher. *The Birdwatcher's Companion: An Encyclopedic Handbook of North American Birdlife.* New York: Hill and Wang, 1982.

Pasquier, Roger F. *Watching Birds.* Boston: Houghton Mifflin, 1977.

Peterson, Roger Tory and the editors of *Life. The Birds.* New York: Time, Inc., 1963.

Sparks, John. *Bird Behavior.* New York: Bantam Books, Grosset and Dunlap, 1970.

Stokes, Donald W. *A Guide to the Behavior of Common Birds.* Boston: Little, Brown and Company, 1979.

Stokes, Donald W. and Lillian Q. *A Guide to Bird Behavior,* vols. 2 and 3. Boston: Little, Brown and Company, 1983 and 1989.

Terres, John K. *Songbirds in Your Garden,* 3rd ed. New York: Hawthorn Books, 1977.

Welty, Joel Carl. *The Life of Birds.* Philadelphia: W. B. Saunders, 1975.

Identification Guides

Peterson, Roger Tory. *A Field Guide to Western Birds,* 4th ed. Boston: Houghton Mifflin, 1980.

———. *A Field Guide To Eastern Birds,* 4th ed. Boston: Houghton Mifflin, 1980.

———. *A Field Guide to the Birds of Texas.* Boston: Houghton Mifflin, 1960.

Robins, Chandler S., Bertel Bruun, and H. S. Zim. *Birds of North America.* New York: Golden Press, 1966.

Walton, Richard K. *Backyard Birdsong.* Boston: Houghton Mifflin, 1991.

———. *Birding By Ear: Eastern.* Boston: Houghton Mifflin, 1989.

———. *Birding By Ear: Western.* Boston: Houghton Mifflin, 1990.

Activities Involving Children with Birds

Earth Works Group. *50 Simple Things You Can Do to Save the Earth*. Berkeley, California: Earthworks Press, 1989.

———— *50 Simple Things Children Can Do to Save the Earth*. Berkeley, California: Earthworks Press, 1990.

Morris, Arthur. "Teaching Children About Birds," *Bird Watcher's Digest*. Jan/Feb 90, Vol. 12 No. 3.

Shuttlesworth, Dorothy. *Exploring Nature with Your Child*. New York: Harry N. Abrams, Inc., 1977.

Nonfiction Written for Children

Cole, Joanna. *A Bird's Body*. New York: William Morrow and Company, 1982.

Cox, Rosamund Kidman and Barbara Cork. *Birds, Usborne First Nature Books*. London: Usborne Publishing Limited, 1980.

Forsyth, Adrian and Laurel Aziz. *Exploring the World of Birds: An Equinox Guide to Avian Life*. Camden, Ontario: Camden House, 1990.

Hickman, Pamela M. *Birdwise: Forty Fun Feats for Finding Out About Our Feathered Friends*. Reading, Massachusetts: Addison-Wesley Publishing Company, Inc., 1989.

Lewis, Barbara A. *The Kid's Guide to Social Action: How to Solve the Social Problems You Choose—and Turn Creative Thinking into Positive Action*. Minneapolis, Minnesota: Free Spirit Publishing Incorporated, 1991.

MacPherson, Mary. *A Young Person's Introduction to Birding*. Toronto: Summerhill Press, 1988.

Rinard, Judith E. *Wildlife Making a Comeback: How Humans Are Helping*. New York: Books for World Explorers National Geographic Society, 1987.

Slide Collections

Cornell Laboratory of Ornithology, Visual Services, 159 Sapsucker Woods Road, Ithaca, NY 14850

Visual Resources for Ornithology (VIREO), Academy of Natural Science, 19th and the Parkway, Philadelphia, PA 19103

Videos

Attracting Birds to Your Backyard (with Roger Tory Peterson), Nature Science Network, Inc. 108 High Street, Carrboro, NC 27510 (60 minutes).

Magazines

Audubon Magazine and *Audubon Field Notes*, National Audubon Society, 1130 Fifth Ave., New York, NY 10028

Bird Watcher's Digest, P.O. Box 110, Marietta, OH 45750

Birder's World: The Magazine for Bird Enthusiasts, Birder's World, Inc., 720 East 8th Street, Holland, MI, 49423

The Living Bird Quarterly, Cornell Laboratory of Ornithology, 159 Sapsucker Woods Road, Ithaca, NY 14850

WildBird, Your Guide to Birding at Its Best, Fancy Publications, Inc., 3 Burroughs, Irvine, CA 92718

Natural History Magazine, American Museum of Natural History, Central Park West at 79th Street, New York, NY 10024

Addresses: Places to Write for More Information

(Most of these organizations will suggest that you become a member. Try to join as many as possible. You will receive educational newsletters, and your money will help them do their work.)

Canadian Nature Federation, 453 Sussex Drive, Ottawa, Ontario, Canada K1N 6Z4

Environmental Defense Fund, 1616 P Street NW, Suite 150, Washington, D.C. 20036

Garbage Magazine, P.O. Box 56519, Boulder, CO 80322

Greenpeace, 1436 U Street NW, Washington, D.C. 20009

Massachusetts Audubon Society, Public Information Office, Great Road, Lincoln, MA 01173

National Audubon Society, 950 Third Avenue, New York, NY 10022

National Wildlife Federation Backyard Wildlife Habitat Program, 1412 16th Street NW, Washington, D.C. 20036-2266

Nature Conservancy, 1815 North Lynn Street, Arlington, VA 22209

The Rainforest Action Network, 301 Broadway, Suite A, San Francisco, CA 94133

Rocky Mountain Institute, 1739 Snowmass Creek Road, Snowmass, CO 81654

Sierra Club, 730 Polk Street, San Francisco, CA 94009

Worldwatch Institute, 1776 Massachusetts Avenue NW, Washington, D.C. 20013

World Wildlife Fund, 1250 24th Street NW, Washington, D.C. 20037

Index

Activity Index